# IN A PERFECT WORLD

## Bermuda in the Context of American Landscape Painting

*Judith Bookbinder*

McMullen Museum of Art
Boston College

This publication is issued in conjunction with the exhibition
*In a Perfect World: Bermuda in the Context of American Landscape Painting,*
curated by Judith Bookbinder and organized by the Charles S. and
Isabella V. McMullen Museum of Art, Boston College
in collaboration with the Masterworks Foundation, Bermuda.

May 16 to September 15, 2002



ISBN 1–892850–03–6

Exhibition and Publication Coordination by Thea Keith-Lucas
Copyediting by Naomi Blumberg and Thea Keith-Lucas
Designer: Keith Ake   Art Director: Andrew Capitos
Produced by the Office of Marketing and Communications
at Boston College   OMC # 2011

Cover:
Winslow Homer (1836-1910)
*Inland Waters,* 1901
Watercolor on paper, 13.75 x 21 in.
The Masterworks Foundation, Bermuda

This exhibition is presented by Fidelity Investments through
the Fidelity Foundation and the FIL Foundation, Bermuda.

Fidelity Investments®

Massachusetts Cultural Council

# CONTENTS


5 PREFACE

7 INTRODUCTION: BERMUDA ON THE MIND

8 IDEALIZED IMAGES OF THE AMERICAN LANDSCAPE

17 BERMUDA AS A NEXUS OF THE REAL AND THE IDEAL

27 ENDNOTES

31 PLATES OF SELECTED WORKS IN THE EXHIBITION

53 LIST OF WORKS IN THE EXHIBITION

# PREFACE



CONCEIVED IN THE WAKE of the tragic events of September 11, 2001, this book and the exhibition that it accompanies examine the thesis that American painters in the nineteenth and early twentieth centuries turned to idealized landscapes for comfort during troublesome times both in their own land and on the nearby, idyllic island of Bermuda. As Utopian and other social reformers, Transcendentalists, and Swedenborgians sought balance through attention to human and spiritual needs, so artists turned to nature to provide a place of refuge in a conflicted world. Beginning with works by artists of the Hudson River School, through Luminist, Tonalist, and Impressionist interpretations, to twentieth-century paintings influenced by Cubist form and Fauve color, this exhibition traces how American artists used various strategies to discover stability, order, and tranquility in nature.

The genesis of this exhibition came about as a truly collaborative confluence of good ideas presented to us by several key groups of people and brought together by our chief curator Alston Conley. First, John and Jacqueline McMullen had encouraged us to organize an exhibition of paintings by George Inness. They introduced us to the director, Patterson Sims, and the curator, Gail Stavitsky, of the Montclair Art Museum, who generously agreed to loan works from their collection. Our Museum Patrons' Committee had suggested an exhibition of American landscape paintings, which are so well represented in our own permanent collection and those of our alumni. At the same time, Tom Butterfield, the founding chairman, and Elise Outerbridge, the curator of the Bermuda Masterworks Foundation presented us with the possibility of showing works from the Foundation's collection of paintings.

We then asked Professor Judith Bookbinder, a scholar of American painting in the Fine Arts department at Boston College, to serve as curator for an exhibition that would look at works assembled from these various sources from a new perspective. It was she who conceived the thesis explored here. She selected the paintings and wrote this catalogue. Her vision, energy and intelligence permeate all aspects of this project; to her we extend our deepest thanks and congratulations.

This endeavor benefited from the help of many who assisted in various ways with research and loans: Christa Balderacchi, Mark and Jennifer Brock, C. Michael Daley, Leah and Alec Petro, John Slavin; Tom Butterfield and Elise Outerbridge (Bermuda Masterworks Foundation); Patterson Sims, Gail Stavitsky, Renee Powley, Margaret Molnar, and Toni Liquori (Montclair Art Museum); Adam Weinberg, Susan Faxon, and Denise Johnson (Addison Gallery of American Art, Phillips Academy), and Malcolm Rogers, Sue Reed, Clifford Ackley, Christopher Atkins, Patricia Loiko, and Kim Pashko (Museum of Fine Arts, Boston).



The staff of the McMullen Museum and others from across the University also contributed to this project. Our chief curator, Alston Conley aided in the selection of works and designed the installation; our exhibitions and publications coordinator Dorothea Keith-Lucas oversaw with great efficiency and discernment the editing and production of the catalogue and the loans of paintings; and our administrator, Helen Swartz coordinated all efforts. Further words of appreciation are due Naomi Blumberg for editorial assistance, Andrew Capitos and Keith Ake for the elegant design of the catalogue, Rosanne Pellegrini for publicity, Steven Vedder, Gary Gilbert and Lee Pellegrini for photography, and Lisa Hastings and Gemma Dorsey for assistance in securing funding.

This project could not have been carried out without substantial support from the administration of Boston College, specifically the president William P. Leahy, academic vice-president John Neuhauser, associate dean of faculties Patricia DeLeeuw, and dean of arts and sciences Joseph Quinn. Very generous support provided by Fidelity Investments through the Fidelity Foundation and the FIL Foundation, Bermuda enabled us to turn this idea into a reality. To each of them, I extend a heartfelt vote of thanks. It is our hope that this probing of the beautiful in painting might provide to the viewers of this exhibition and readers of this catalogue the comfort, solace and place of refuge from a troubled world that it did for our ancestors.

Nancy Netzer
Director, McMullen Museum of Art
Professor of Art History, Boston College

# IN A PERFECT WORLD: BERMUDA IN THE CONTEXT OF AMERICAN LANDSCAPE PAINTING

## Introduction: Bermuda on the Mind



WORN OUT BY WHAT he termed “frail nerves”, Marsden Hartley sailed to Bermuda in June 1935. In the midst of the Depression years, the previous winter had been a trying time of personal loss and financial struggle for him. In January, unable to pay the continuing costs of storing his unsold canvases and drawings in a New York warehouse, he had destroyed over one hundred of his works rather than see them auctioned off at distressed prices in a warehouse sale. As he carried out that grim task, he held in his pocket a letter notifying him that his poverty-stricken sister had recently died. By spring, the sale of a painting permitted him to escape the site of such unhappiness, and he immediately left for a place that promised refreshment and renewal. “Bermuda is what it is,” he wrote, “nothing whatever but sunlight—soft air—and the water like thermal baths, and they have soothed me quite a bit.”[1] In this environment, he observed the coral reef that surrounds the island, and he painted *Sunken Treasure.*

In voyaging to a remote island, Hartley was following a pattern that numerous American landscape painters had established in the prior century. They had traveled near and sometimes very far believing that they would find comfort, courage, pride, or strength in nature. In creating *Sunken Treasure* (no. 14), which is at once a transcript of Hartley’s visual experience and a conceptual abstraction, he also connected with the tradition of idealized images of nature. “I have made the complete return to nature,” Hartley had announced in 1928, “and nature is, as we all know, primarily an intellectual idea. I am satisfied that painting also is, like nature, an intellectual idea....”[2] Particularly in times of trouble, whether personal or communal, painters such as Hartley have seen in nature the reflection of their own needs. This exhibition examines how artists have used an idealized form-language to create visual projections of their best hopes “in a perfect world” while recognizing the limitations of the real world.

Painters who journeyed to Bermuda from the last

decade of the nineteenth century and into the twentieth century brought with them a wide variety of stylistic conventions in which they interpreted their experiences of landscape. In styles ranging from Impressionism to Fauvism and Cubism, they created images that ultimately conveyed an idealized sense of order and harmony. This exhibition considers their images in the context of the trajectory of idealized American landscape painting of the nineteenth century, when painters used classical, romantic, naturalistic, and impressionist approaches to construct images that offered comfort to viewers in often troubled times.

## Idealized Images of the American Landscape

LANDSCAPE PAINTING BEGAN in earnest as the country confronted the challenge of defining American national identity. The War of 1812 settled the question of America's independence from Britain, and, with the completion of the Erie Canal in 1825, shipping and commerce extended the country's reach from inland waterways to the Atlantic. The character and extent of the country remained in flux as new states and territories were added to the Union, immigration expanded and diversified the population, and steam technology forecast new industrial possibilities.[3] The debate on national identity paralleled the effort of artists to find images resonant with the needs of society and to develop a coherent sequence of pictorial inventions and responses.[4] The nature of national identity and the nature of American art were situated in the land itself as Americans, in general, and artists, in particular, began to define the United States.



Thomas Doughty (1793–1856) was among the first to paint landscapes with a discernible American character. As early as the 1830s, he set out for Mount Desert Island off the Maine coast to find a place of unspoiled beauty, called by some a "New World Island of Cythera,"[5] and he produced some of the earliest paintings of that isolated landscape. More often, he journeyed to the rural regions of New York State, where he combined the facts he observed with atmospheric effects and classical structure to create pastoral reveries such as *In the Catskills.* Images such as this one established a paradigm for early dialogue on the American landscape.

Ironically, Doughty looked to European models to bring structure and order to his American scenes. Drawing on a formula that had been employed by painters at the court of Louis XIV, particularly Claude Lorraine, Doughty constructed a view of the land of upstate New York in which the observer is invited to proceed along a clear path into a sunlit and tranquil space framed and balanced by feathery trees. As the Sun King had needed to believe that his power was reflected in an orderly world, Doughty's audience was comforted to see its hopes for a harmonious and secure land confirmed in *In the Catskills,* where tiny figures enjoy a picnic in a benevolent and protected landscape.

More topographically specific than *In the Catskills,* Doughty's view of the *Hudson River near West Point* (no.1) became an enduring geographical paradigm and the point of departure for artists who would be identified by that locale regardless of the specific places they chose to record. His painting represents "perhaps the most canonical site of American landscape art," Nicolai Cikovsky states, "a region that would soon become as sanctified for American landscape artists as the Roman Campagna and the forest of Fontainebleau had been for European ones."[6] The Hudson River School became synonymous with images of sweeping breadth that combined the specifics of place with grandeur of vision and idealized perfection often suggesting divine presence.

*Hudson River near West Point* takes the viewer, literally, to a higher plane where the exhilarating vista conjures thoughts of power and possession. From an elevated clearing, the viewer looks down on the river valley and out toward the distant horizon signifying a future of expansive possibility. "The landscape view from the heights," Albert Boime argues, would typify many nineteenth-century American landscape paintings, "revealing in their common structural paradigm the sociopolitical ideology of expansionist thought."[7] Jefferson's purchase of the Louisiana Territory in 1803 inaugurated the campaign for westward expansion under the imprimatur of "Manifest Destiny". This belief that the United States was ordained by God to expand from the Atlantic to the Pacific would serve as the rallying cry as the United States continued to acquire territory throughout the century.

As the United States labored to take its place with the great nation–states of Europe, insecurities about national identity were ameliorated by the belief that the country had the support of divine powers manifested in its land. The metaphoric discourse of much of the nineteenth century was laced with references to the transcendence of the American landscape. "In the woods is perpetual youth," Ralph Waldo Emerson declared. "Within these plantations of God, a decorum and sanctity reign, a perennial festival is dressed, and the guest sees not how he should tire of them in a thousand years." Nature offered not only evidence of God, but also an orderly model for society. "In the woods," Emerson continued, "we return to reason and faith. There I feel that nothing can befall me in life, – no disgrace, no calamity (leaving me my eyes), which nature cannot repair."[8]

Landscape painters turned their tools to creating images expressive of the same divine presence. "The truths of light and atmosphere that absorbed American artists," Barbara Novak observes, "quickly served a concept of nature as God, turning landscape paintings into proto-icons." These landscape/icons were also configured to represent the ideal order of God's handiwork. "[T]he perfect solution," Novak states, "was one that reconciled the real and the ideal, the tangible and the ephemeral, that infused the inviolate 'stuff' of God's world with Godhead."[9]

Thomas Cole (1801–1848), who had emigrated from England to America as a child, took up the challenge of manifesting the presence of God through the specific features of his adopted land. Confident that "those scenes of solitude from which the hand of nature has never been lifted affect the mind with a more deep toned emotion than aught which the hand of man has touched," he set out to create images of unspoiled wilderness, which would inspire "the consequent associations... of God the creator" because their models "are his undefiled works and the mind is cast into the contemplation of eternal things."[10] Thus, Cole climbed the heights near his Catskill home, or in western Massachusetts, or on Mount Desert Island to experience the presence of God in unspoiled nature and to paint works like *View of the Round-top in the Catskill Mountains.*

Cole's friend and "kindred spirit", the poet William Cullen Bryant, described the same exhilarating experience in his poem *Monument Mountain*:

*Thou who wouldst see the lovely and the wild*
*Mingled in harmony on Nature's face,*
*Ascend our rocky mountains. Let thy foot*
*Fail not with weariness, for on their top*
*The beauty and the majesty of earth,*
*Spread wide beneath, shall make thee to forget*
*The steep and toilsome way. There, as thou standest,*
*The haunts of men below thee, and around*
*The mountain summits, thy expanding heart*
*Shall feel a kindred with that loftier world*
*To which thou art translated, and partake*
*The enlargement of thy vision.*[11]

While Bryant was unambiguous in his statement, Cole often left the viewer to wonder about the future. Paintings like *Oxbow of the Connecticut River near Northampton* (fig. 1) raise numerous questions. Will the pastoral land-scape of neatly planted fields and placid rivers dotted with occasional boats continue to coexist with the untamed wilderness? Can God's immanence in nature withstand the onslaught of civilization? Cole soon witnessed the price of progress in his own environment.

When the Erie Canal connected the Great Lakes to the east coast in 1825, most Americans still lived along the eastern seaboard. However, almost immediately railroads began to make the Erie and other canals obsolete as they cut through new territory with hitherto unimagined speed and carried the population westward. Cole could only

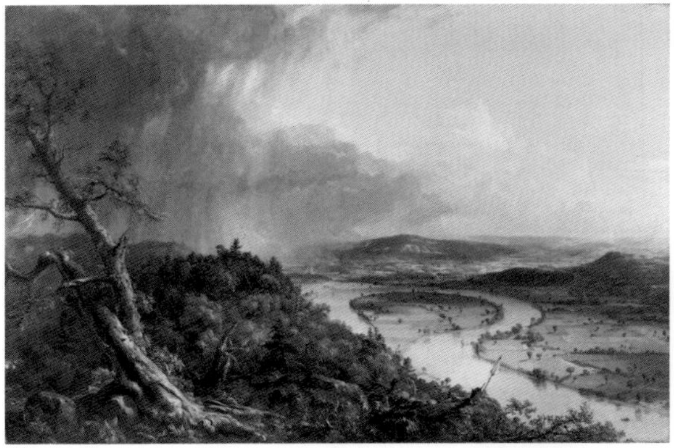

**Fig. 1**
Thomas Cole
*Oxbow of the Conecticut River near Northhampton*
Oil on canvas, 51.5 x 76 in.
The Metropolitan Museum of Art, Gift of Russell Sage, 1908.
08.228

watch helplessly as the Catskill and Canajoharie Railroad began to lay track on land adjacent to his property in 1835. "The copper-hearted barbarians are cutting all the trees down in the beautiful valley on which I have looked so often with a loving eye," Cole lamented to Luman Reed, his patron, in March 1836. "Tell this to Durand," Cole's friend and fellow painter, "not that I wish to give him pain, but that I want him to join me in maledictions on all dollar-godded utilitarians."[12] To express his anger, Cole wrote a poem entitled *The Complaint of the Forest*:

*All then was harmony and peace – but man*
*Arose – he who now vaunts antiquity –*
*He the destroyer – amid the shades*
*Of oriental realms, destruction's work began –*
*And dissonant – the axe – the unresting axe*
*Incessant smote our venerable ranks....*[13]

Throughout the century, artists as diverse as Cole, George Inness, and Winslow Homer would use the image of the axe and the fallen tree as a metaphor for the cost of progress. The following year, as if to defy reality, Cole painted *View on the Catskill—Early Autumn* (fig. 2) in which he ignored the presence of the railroad in his backyard. Cole's construction of a fictive scene that transformed the facts of reality into an idealized and more appealing image of pastoral progress established a precedent that other members of the Hudson River School and their descendants would follow.

For much of the nineteenth century, Jasper Cropsey (1823–1900) approached nature in the Hudson River School manner utilizing precisely rendered details to construct idealized images of an expansive landscape bathed in ethereal light. Born on Staten Island, he traveled throughout New Jersey, New York, and New England gathering site-specific material to transform into panoramic visions. His *Landscape* of 1875 abandons the framed Claudian formula for an open, strongly horizontal composition that leads the viewer through a closely delineated foreground, where a cottage stands almost lost in soft shadow, into a broadly painted sunlit distance. As Susan Faxon has observed, Cropsey's idyllic image of the lush American countryside testifies to "the happy accommodation of nature and man."[14] In "Up among the Clouds", an essay he wrote in 1855 for *The Crayon*, Cropsey revealed his penchant for finding idealized vistas even in the sky. "Grand masses of dreamy forms floating by each other, sometimes looking like magic palaces, rising higher and higher, and then toppling over in deep valleys, to rise again in ridges like snowy mountains," reminded him that, "In boyhood, we have often watched this dream-world, and peopled it with angels [and] in manhood, from the cares of life we have turned, and been refreshed by the glimpses of its 'silver lining.'"[15] In drawing larger meaning from detailed observation, Cropsey was unifying Cole's vision with Asher Durand's advice, which had also appeared in *The Crayon* in 1855, that the painter should "go first to Nature to paint landscape".[16]

As he explored the wilderness in search of an ideal America, John Casilear (1811–1893) was also drawn to combine Cole's more conceptual and Durand's more visual approaches. While maintaining a highly successful business in New York that specialized in banknote engraving, Casilear was also able to study painting with Durand who was Casilear's life-long friend and mentor. In fact, in 1831 Durand purchased Casilear's first significant landscape painting, and nine years later Casilear traveled to Europe for the first time with Durand and two other painters, John Kensett and Thomas Rossiter. The group was particularly impressed with the Claude Lorraine paintings they saw in Paris.[17] The richness of these landscapes was a revelation because, like most art students in America, Casilear and his friends had only seen engraved illustrations of the European paintings they emulated. Casilear's *Hudson River Scene* (no. 15) transposes the Clau-

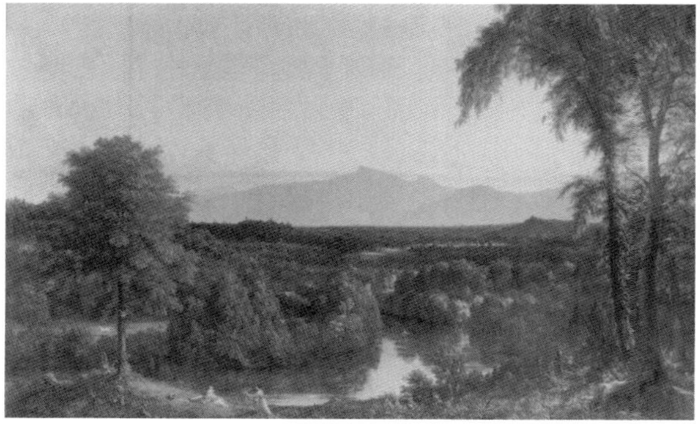

Fig. 2
Thomas Cole
*View on the Catskill—*
*Early Autumn*, 1837
Oil on canvas, 39 x 63 in
The Metropolitan Museum of Art, Gift in memory of Jonathan Sturges by his children, 1895
95.13.3

dian model into a localized North American site. Feathery trees in a shadowed foreground create an asymmetric frame that beckons the viewer to enter the space and move gradually along the waterway, into the soft pastel planes of the distance, to a pink horizon.

Here Casilear presents the double message of the Hudson River School: that humanity can rejoice in the harmony of nature as seen in the American wilderness, and, at the same time, occupy that benign wilderness without altering its balance. This message resonated in the intense atmosphere of the 1840s when the annexation of Texas, the settling of the Oregon Territory border dispute with Canada, and the end of the war with Mexico expanded the United States to the Pacific Ocean. This growth inaugurated fierce debates over whether that vast landscape would be developed and whether slavery would be permitted in the various territories and new states. Amid the public scramble for land rights and political control, artists blazed trails for others to follow from the Catskills to California. "The summer of 1849 was spent by Messrs. Casilear and Kensett at Haines Falls and Kaaterskill Clove," a newspaper reported, "and their ladders and paths were the first by which that portentous gorge was rendered easy of access."[18] The images they produced would also encourage others to follow.

Benjamin Champney (1817–1907) joined the same intrepid group to explore New England in the 1850s and settled permanently in a house and studio on the main street of North Conway, New Hampshire. By that time, the valleys surrounding the White Mountains were becoming easily accessible by railroad from Boston and New York, and by 1853 forty painters were working in North Conway. In spite of the changes in the area, Champney's paintings perpetuated the image of pristine wilderness and minimal pastoral development.[19] In his painting of *Mote Mountain from Walker's Pond* (no. 16), he applied the Claudian bucolic formula to an intimate foreground space in an unusual vertical format. The rocky banks of a small inlet with gossamer trees frame a view of the distant mountain lying low on the horizon. Silvery light suffuses the atmosphere binding the calm waters and clear sky in a harmony of cool tones. In this work, the linear clarity and realistic detail of the earlier Hudson River School painters give way to generalized forms in an overall tonality. Its new quiet and contemplative mood signals a change in American landscape painting that has been termed Luminist. While the vertical orientation of Champney's painting is unusual for the Luminist style, which generally has a strong horizontal emphasis and an open, unframed composition, its expressive light and total stillness exhibit the salient features of Luminism.

Luminism evolved in an era of doubt and crisis in the 1850s and '60s as the nation stridently declared its territorial mandate while factional disputes undermined its integrity. In response, Transcendentalists called for silence and more intimate communion with God in nature. "Those divine sounds which are uttered to our inward ear," Henry David Thoreau noted, "which are breathed in with the zephyr or reflected from the lake—come to us noiselessly, bathing the temples of the soul, as we stand motionless amid the rocks. The halloo is the creature of walls and mason-work; the whisper is fitted in the depths of the wood, or by the shore of the lake; but silence is best adapted to the acoustics of space."[20]

Painters took the lead in projecting the image of peace so that, by late 1860, *The Crayon* could report, "Notwithstanding the political commotion, the art world pursues the even tenor of its ways. Artists are now busy in their studios with the harmonies of nature, not its discords. We cannot help but think that the general cultivation of artistic feeling and perception would be of great political advantage."[21]

George Loring Brown (1814–1889) subordinated the details of his *View of Norwalk Islands, Norwalk, Connecticut* (no. 17) to the overall stillness and horizontality of this panoramic Luminist view where humanity and nature reside "in cultivated harmony".[22] The figure of the fisherman in the left foreground is scaled to a space that contains but does not overwhelm him. He, the sailboats that dot the calm, coastal waters, and the tree at the far right are vertical counterweights in perfect balance with the horizon line. Brown achieved a classical equilibrium, similar to Dutch landscape painting in its structure, which may have served as a source of inspiration for some of the Luminists as they searched for visual metaphors of security in the period of the Civil War.[23]

No painter was more in need of solace than Sanford Gifford (1823–1880), who saw active service at the front and lost his two brothers in the Union cause. Charles was killed in an early battle in 1861. Edward was captured during the Battle of New Orleans in 1863 when he volunteered for a dangerous mission. He escaped by swimming across the Mississippi River but later contracted typhoid fever and died.[24] In 1864, Gifford returned to his studio in the Tenth Street Studio Building in New York, but he soon left for Mount Desert, Maine as Doughty and Cole had done before him. Unlike his predecessors, however, Gifford traveled to this still relatively isolated island to find healing, rather than exaltation, in nature. His *Lake Scene—Mountain Background* (no. 2), painted after his trip to Maine, reflects his effort to transcend the specifics of site and to idealize the "forest primeval". The tight linearity of Brown's rendering of the Norwalk coast gives way here to a golden glow that dissolves detail and unifies an unframed and limitless space. Loose, painterly, quasi-impressionist brushstrokes suggest evanescent form presaging Gifford's later comment that, "the really important matter is not the natural object itself, but the veil or medium through which we see it."[25]

During the Civil War, in works such as *Approaching Storm, Beach at Newport,* Martin Johnson Heade (1819–1904) depicted the coasts and marshes of Rhode Island and Massachusetts with darkening skies and the stillness of imminent danger. His later paintings, *Sailing by Moonlight* (no. 18) and *Low Clouds over a Marsh,* contain the same classical structure of strong horizontal lines punctuated sparingly by a lone sailboat or a few isolated haystacks that had characterized his paintings of the 1860s. Yet in both the more linear coastal scene and the more impressionistic marsh scene, the tension and foreboding of the wartime landscapes have given way to serenity. The glowing circle of moonlight and its reflection form a vertical path drawing the viewer into the cool blue horizontal space of *Sailing by Moonlight.* In *Low Clouds over a Marsh,* Heade again used light, here a warm rosy tonality, to unify the unbroken line of the horizon and the vertical rhythms of marsh grass, haystacks, and distant trees. Only the softly scumbled clouds provide tonal contrast, although they still reinforce the horizontality of the composition.

Thomas Moran (1837–1926) was able to find perfect balance and classical order in small-scaled landscape, particularly near his home on Long Island and while traveling through Florida. Although his operatic depictions of the vast spaces of the West responded to the expansionist call of Manifest Destiny through the 1870s, Moran's later paintings present nature in a quieter and nostalgic mood. Moving back in time and space, the rowboats gliding along an inland waterway in *On the St. John's River* (no. 19) allude to earlier days of river transport that had largely been replaced by the age of steam. The muted tones and painterly rendering seem to capture Samuel Clemens's nostalgic vision as Huckleberry Finn describes dawn as seen on a river raft: "Not a sound, anywheres – perfectly still – just like the whole world was asleep, only sometimes the bull-frogs a-cluttering, maybe. The first thing to see, looking away over the water, was a kind of dull line – that was the woods on t'other side – you couldn't make nothing else out; then a pale place in the sky; then more paleness, spreading around; then the river softening up, away off, and warn't black any more, but gray...."[26] In Moran's painting the forms of the riverbanks emerge from a delicate haze along a low horizon line punctuated by discrete vertical elements inviting the viewer to glide smoothly into the plane of the river.

This voyage back in time as well as space was a recurring theme for artists confronted with an increasingly industrialized world. "[T]echnology, at first a thrilling agent in the romance of science," John Wilmerding notes, "now was a disquieting invader of nature's paradise."[27] George Inness (1825–1894) began his career by saluting progress in paintings of *The Delaware Water Gap* (fig. 3) and *Lackawanna Valley*, in which railroad trains steam into Claudian landscapes of the Hudson River School mode. However, Inness adopted an increasingly idealized and abstract mode of rendering nature as he sought to rise above material reality. "He uses nature's forms," a critic noted about Inness in 1863, "simply as a language to express thought."[28] Under the influence of his early patron, the Protestant minister and abolitionist Henry Ward Beecher, Inness began to distill the raw material of the natural world to its formal and conceptual essence. Beecher declared Inness to be "the first of American painters" and admonished that, "he will see the most without, who has the most within," adding, "he who only sees with his bodily organs sees but surfaces."[29] Throughout his career, Inness heeded Beecher's advice and sought to penetrate to the spiritual core of nature.

When Inness traveled to Paris in 1853, he encountered paintings that reinforced his approach to landscape. He identified with contemporary French artists who left their urban studios to paint the bucolic scenery around the village of Barbizon in the Fontainbleau forest. Although these Barbizon painters worked en plein air, they orchestrated light and idealized form to interpret rather than imitate the landscape they observed.

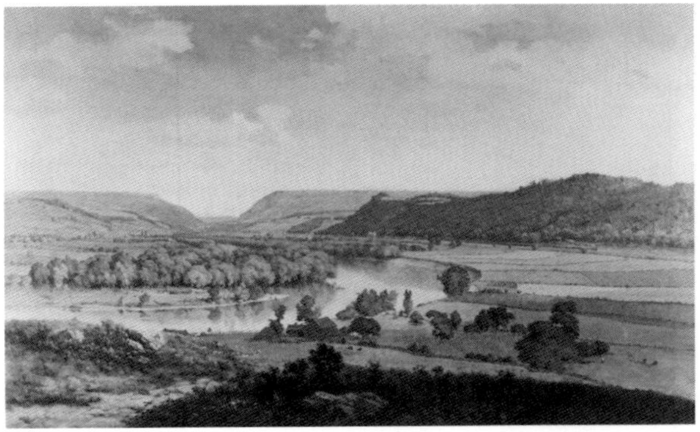

Fig. 3
George Inness (1825–1894)
*The Delaware Water Gap*, 1857
Oil on canvas, 32 x 52.25 in.
The Montclair Art Museum
Gift of Mrs. F.G. Herman Fayen
30.2

Like the Barbizon painters, Inness left his urban home to find a more peaceful working environment. His early years, including some brief art instruction and an apprenticeship with an engraving firm, had been spent in New Jersey and New York City. As a chronic epileptic condition worsened in 1859, he decided to move to the quiet rural village of Medfield, Massachusetts. Peter Bermingham notes that the Medfield stay "brought him the sort of physical and emotional relief he constantly sought throughout his career."[30] During that three-year period, he began to assemble a vocabulary of key motifs from which he could draw at will to construct images of the refuge he sought in nature. Open, rolling fields interrupted by sometimes one, sometimes several trees, and bordered by a distant line of trees define the basic format of *Medfield Landscape* (no. 20), *Summer Landscape*, and *Autumn Landscape*. Color differences of fields and skies connote the character and temperature of the seasons from the cool crisp spring-like blues and greens of the first of these paintings, to the golden tones of the second, to the touches of red and orange in the third. Even the later, more generalized *Late Afternoon*, with its wispy, attenuated trees and diffused light, recalls the same underlying formula.

From the Medfield years onward, Inness constructed idealized landscapes of classical balance and order by using increasingly broadly defined, open horizontal planes punctuated by isolated vertical elements. The term Tonalist is often applied to these subtle, quiet works that capture the introspection of his conversion to Swedenborgianism in 1867. Emanuel Swedenborg, an eighteenth-century scientist, claimed that direct empirical experience of the spiritual world proved the continuity of the material and spiritual realms. His platonic view appealed to many nineteenth-century American intellectuals inspired by various manifestations of idealism from education reform, to abolition, temperance, and Transcendentalism. "In Swedenborg," Inness's son observed, "George Inness found the basis for his theory of art.... To him all nature was symbolic – full of spiritual meaning."[31] Even the topographical features of *Old Aqueduct, Campagna, Rome,* painted as a commercial venture during his second trip to Europe in the early 1870s, transcend the typical tourist view to become a meditation on light and time. *Sunset Glow* (no. 3) manifests the Tonalist reductivism of Inness's late works and his efforts to use natural forms to reach a higher spirituality. His poem *Exaltation* captured this effort:

*Verse I:* *Sing joyfully!*
*Earth-bound no more,*
*We rise,*
*Creation speaks anew*
*In brighter tones.*
*Life now enthrones*
*Its imaged forms,*
*Winged with a joy that*
*Ne'er from nature grew.*[32]

In painting *Sunset Glow,* Inness achieved a transcendental fusion of the subjective and objective and trembled on the brink of abstraction.

In the meantime, other painters such as Dwight Tryon (1849–1925) adopted Inness's more personal approach to landscape.[33] As Inness had before him, Tryon traveled to France and gravitated toward the poetic plein-air painting of the Barbizon artists. Leaving the rigidity of the Paris academies, Tryon moved to Auvers, north of Paris, to work with Charles-François Daubigny, one of the few remaining original Barbizon painters. There, Tryon painted *Twilight at Auvers*, a work that is more representational than Inness's *Sunset Glow*, but similar to it in structure and transcendental spirit. The ethereal brushwork and introspective mood of these paintings stand in quiet opposition to the growing materialism in America in the later decades of the nineteenth century.

Tryon had traveled to Europe, as many American painters and writers did, partially to find artistic inspiration and partially to escape the onslaught of materialism at home. He knew that European subjects appealed to the taste of newly rich patrons who were bored with images of local sites and wanted paintings that would attest to their newly acquired sophistication. Whatever Tryon's assessment of his patrons may have been, the editor of *The Nation* typified those writers who were appalled by this arriviste cultural elite. He declared that the United States was a "gaudy stream of bespangled, belaced, and beruffled barbarians" and asked and answered: "Who knows how to be rich in America? Plenty of people know how to get money; but... to be rich properly is, indeed, a fine art. It requires culture, imagination, and character,"[34] qualities hard to find at home in the late nineteenth century. "Many Americans," historian Samuel P. Hays observed, "drew back in disgust before the crudeness of the new age and the graft, corruption, praise of material values, and destruction of resources which accompanied it."[35] Tryon's increasingly idealized and dematerialized later landscapes seemed to offer an alternative to this rampant materialism. In a similar way, the Utopian movement and the plethora of Utopian novels it spawned in the later nineteenth century, particularly Edward Bellamy's *Looking Backward* (1888), gave voice to those who believed that a more perfect society was a possibility.[36] Artists and writers took every opportunity to explore new models for social transformation or, at least, for cultural and formal inspiration.



John La Farge (1835–1910) eagerly accepted Henry Adams's invitation to join him on a tour of Japan, which promised a paradise unspoiled by the technology of the West. As their ship entered Yokohama harbor on July 3, 1886, the natural beauty of the scene stunned La Farge. "We are coming in," he wrote in his handcrafted book, *An Artist's Letters from Japan*, "it is like the picture books. Anything I can add will only be a filling in of detail."[37] He included in his book drawings and watercolors of temples, landscape, and people he encountered, and he described his visits to the Iyeyasu and Iyemitsu shrines on the holy mountain of Nikko. In spite of the impressiveness of the structures, the natural features of Nikko inspired his strongest responses. "As we turn to the highest court on the left and ascend slowly steep, high steps to a gorgeous red gate above our heads, whose base we cannot see," he observed that, "the great cedars of the opposite side are the real monuments...."[38] In *Landscape in Nikko*, he positioned the monumental cedars as the anchor of a composition of simplified planes that simultaneously represent atmospheric distance and flat surfaces in perfect balance. La Farge's painting demonstrated that the tranquility of the remote and exotic islands of Japan, available only to the inveterate western traveler, could be reconstituted in the image and enjoyed vicariously by the viewer.

Other late nineteenth-century painters and writers chose to look closer at hand for sites of refuge. The poet Celia Laughton Thaxter found Appledore Island, one of the Isles of Shoals, ten miles off the New Hampshire coast near Portsmouth. "The island itself," Barbara Weinberg observes, "was a place detached from the new urban life and reassuringly identified – like Thaxter herself and her poetry – with the very bedrock of old New England and earlier America."[39] Thaxter's house on Appledore attracted painters, writers, and musicians eager to escape the city heat of summer and to enjoy the camaraderie of an artists' colony amid the austere remoteness of these islands. Childe Hassam (1859–1935) was among those eager to share Thaxter's hospitality and the refuge of Appledore. Even after her death in 1894, he returned to the island where he painted *Morning Calm, Appledore* (no. 4). The simplified planes of the rocky island, the calm water, and pale summer sky recall the organization and harmony of Luminist and Tonalist paintings, although the almost square canvas configures the image in a new way.

New, too, are the sparkle of light, the broken brushstroke, and the optical realism that reflect Hassam's absorption of the Impressionist approach. Hassam, who was born in Dorchester, Massachusetts and was the son of a wealthy merchant, had access at an early age to art instruction and foreign travel. In the 1880s, he studied at the Académie Julien in Paris, set up a studio near Place Pigalle, and learned at first hand about the experiments of the French Impressionists. He brought their ideas on rendering light and landscape back to the United States in 1889, staying briefly in Boston before settling in New York. From there, he traveled during summers sometimes to Cos Cob or Old Lyme, Connecticut or to Gloucester, Massachusetts, but he also returned to Appledore's isolated tranquility.



## Bermuda as a Nexus of the Real and the Ideal

AS DOUGHTY HAD EXPLORED Mount Desert Island, La Farge had voyaged to Japan, and Hassam had traveled to Appledore, numerous American as well as Canadian and European painters came to Bermuda. They found, and continue to find, islands to be particularly engaging as places of escape from the cares of civilization. Bermuda's low green landscape enfolded by a current of Gulf Stream air is "an oasis of warmth in a cold and seemingly endless sea,"[40] a reality and a metaphor that would resonate particularly for artists confronting the physical hardships of northern environments. The island would attract American and European travelers with its unique combination of the exotic and the familiar. Its landscape of tropical turquoise water, pink sand, majestic palms, and red and pink hibiscus and oleander is inflected with winding roads, dark pines, and rocky promontories that recall Cornwall in England or the coast of Maine.

Yet, Bermuda was not always perceived as a salubrious refuge. The cluster of islands that would become Britain's oldest self-ruling colony was named for its Spanish discoverer, Juan de Bermudez, and first appeared on a map drawn by Peter Martyr in 1511. However, the formidable seas crashing against the surrounding reefs so "affrighted and dismaied" the sailors voyaging between the Old and New Worlds that they called it the "Isle of Devils" and avoided the area as much as possible for the remainder of the sixteenth century.[41] That reputation changed forever in July 1609 when Admiral Sir George Somers miraculously brought the *Sea Venture,* his foundering ship full of English passengers bound for the fledgling colony of Virginia, to rest off Bermuda's rocky shore.

From that time, Bermuda would continue to be perceived as an elusive utopian paradise. Thirteen years after the passengers of the *Sea Venture* set foot on the island's pink-tinted sands, a character in a play by the English playwright, Thomas Middleton, declared, "E'en to seek out a quiet life, my lord: I do hear of a fine peaceable island.... Gentlemen, I am for the Bermudas."[42] A century later, John Smibert, a young Scottish-born artist working in London, jumped at the opportunity to become drawing instructor at the college the Protestant churchman Dean George Berkeley intended to establish in Bermuda. The Berkeley entourage landed at Newport, Rhode Island in 1728 to await Parliament's approval of funds for the enterprise, a wait that would be in vain. The only lasting outcome of the project is Smibert's portrait of what came to be called the *Bermuda Group,* an early testimony to an idealistic vision often associated with the island.

For Winslow Homer (1836–1910), Bermuda certainly seemed the antithesis of his home environment at Prout's Neck, Maine – at least in the wintertime – and he rendered the island with a classical order very different from the tension characteristic of most of his other work. Even his trips to the Bahamas produced images of men battling the forces of nature, culminating at the close of the nineteenth century in the heroic struggle of *The Gulf Stream* (fig. 4). The paintings of Bermuda, however, construct a landscape of balance and serenity with only a few suggestions of movement.

Born and raised in Boston, Homer began his training in a lithography workshop there and earned freelance illustration assignments for *Balou's Pictorial Drawing-Room Companion* and *Harper's Weekly.*[43] A commission from *Harper's* in 1862 to travel with the Union Army and send back the first images of the Civil War set the stage for his lifelong interest in human struggle, a subject that he explored with few interruptions except for the Bermuda visits. Samuel Clemens's quip that "Bermuda is heaven but you have to go through hell to get there"[44] probably characterizes Homer's experience of the island.

Homer's first trip to Bermuda came at a pivotal moment in his career and at a universal moment of transition. The final year of the nineteenth century began on a high note for him with the sale in February of Thomas Clarke's collection of his work, which set record-breaking



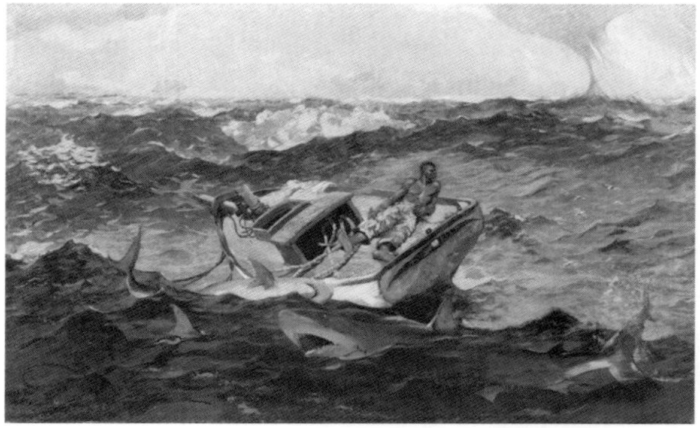

Fig. 4
Winslow Homer (1836–1910)
*The Gulf Stream*
Oil on canvas
28.125 x 49.125 in.
The Metropolitan Museum of Art, Wolfe Fund, 1906
Catherine Lorillard Wolfe Collection. 06.1234

prices and enormously enhanced his reputation, and concluded with the completion of *The Gulf Stream* in December.[45] That monumental work was, as John Wilmerding states, "an embodiment of the fin-de-siècle mood of anxiety, if not despair, felt by many in America and Europe in these years." Wilmerding goes on to characterize the period as "an age of transition, as Homer's near contemporary Henry Adams was to articulate in his *Education*, published in 1906, and Albert Einstein was to confirm with his theory of relativity, announced about the same time. Both art and science, by means of Picasso's cubism, the technology of the X ray, and the practice of psychoanalysis, were about to dissect and penetrate the surface of the visible world."[46] At that pregnant moment, Homer rewarded himself with a trip to Bermuda.

Sailing to the island for the first time on the *S.S. Trinidad*, he arrived in Hamilton harbor on December 8, 1899 and stayed until January 22, 1900. The stark, almost monochromatic washes of his painting, *S.S. Trinidad, Bermuda*, record his voyage and presage the dramatic clarity of vision and reductive organization he would bring to his Bermuda works. He returned to the island in 1901, and the two visits yielded nineteen known watercolor paintings of beautiful vistas rendered in saturated jewel-like colors applied in broad washes.[47] The Bermuda watercolors mark the pinnacle of Homer's achievement in the medium, unifying his mood of spontaneous joy expressed in brilliant light and color with a resolved sense of order. On the island, he painted, as Wilmerding concludes, "some of the most free, lush, intimate, and subtle works of his maturity."[48] In a 1902 letter to his dealer, Homer declared these paintings to be "as good work...as I ever did."[49] Certainly they evidence Homer's positive frame of mind in Bermuda.

In *Inland Water* (no. 5) and *Rocky Shore, Bermuda*, Homer tackled very different landscape situations but arrived at peaceful resolutions in both cases. He painted *Inland Water* on a calm winter's day looking out to Granaway Deep in the Great Sound from above Harbour Road. The immediacy of the foreground plane and its warm tonality set the stage for a series of dissolving planes of bright, cool color moving into the distance and upward on the surface. The simple geometry of the block-like pink and yellow cottages contrasts with the insistent horizontals of sea, outlying land, and sky, and the result is perfect balance. With the absence of human activity, the only movement is in Homer's scumbled paint passages in the foreground and blotting in the clouds. In *Rocky Shore, Bermuda*, he caught the choppy tide as it strikes an outcropping of stratified rock along the open ocean shoreline. The erosion process cut an arch in the rock, which becomes an oval of light when the formation is reflected in the surrounding water. The immediate foreground plane of sand and dark foliage balances this moment of drama. The action of the choppy waves near the shore is resolved in the insistent horizontality of the sea. When Homer was asked if he agreed that beauty is essentially everywhere in nature, waiting to be seized by the artist, he replied: "Yes, but the rare thing is to find a painter who knows a good thing when he sees it. You must wait...patiently until the exceptional, the wonderful affect or aspect comes."[50] Homer seems to have followed his own advice in these paintings.

Other artists who came to Bermuda at the end of the nineteenth century and in the early decades of the twentieth century often followed stylistic trails that they had blazed in other places. Frank Bicknell (1866–1943), for example, was part of the American Impressionist group, including Childe Hassam, who usually spent their summers painting the sparkle of light on the countryside near Old Lyme, Connecticut. Although he made his home in Connecticut for forty years, Bicknell also yearned for the romantic paradise and sailed to Japan, as La Farge and others had done. Stopping in Bermuda in 1894 on his return from the Far East, he painted *Souvenir of Bermuda*. Its loosely brushed strokes of delicate color testify to his Impressionist roots, while its simplified foreground plane and strong horizontal orientation punctuated with selective vertical accents reveal the influence of prints he would have seen during his visit to Japan.



Ross Sterling Turner (1847–1915) also joined Hassam's circle and vacationed at Celia Thaxter's home on Appledore Island in 1883, about the same time he began visiting Bermuda. The short, choppy, and brightly colored strokes of his watercolor and gouache painting, *Fairylands, Bermuda* characterize his Impressionist rendering of an idealized setting. At the same time, the subtly modulated translucent planes of his Bermuda images are similar to Inness's Tonalist approach.

Thomas Anshutz (1851–1912), as student and assistant to the staunch realist Thomas Eakins at the Pennsylvania Academy of Fine Arts in Philadelphia, would seem to have been an unlikely exponent of the idealized Bermuda landscape. However, he and his friend and fellow artist Edmund Greacen were also drawn to the Old Lyme Impressionist group where they knew Bicknell. Anshutz had met Greacen after that painter had returned from Giverny.[51] Anshutz succeeded Eakins as director of the Pennsylvania Academy in 1909, and the following year he and Greacen went to Bermuda. The loose brushwork and saturated color of the Impressionists is apparent in Anshutz's oil painting, *South Shore, Bermuda* (no. 6). However, as with Homer's Bermuda renderings, Anshutz achieved an idealized monumentality by reducing his composition to a few visual elements. The generalized color masses of the foreground shoreline culminate in the dark, spiky pines, whose trunks and branches seem to point toward the placid horizon line that unifies the composition and declares the stability of the scene.

Charles Hawthorne (1872–1930) carried to Bermuda the Impressionist focus on color and light he had developed as a student and assistant of William Merritt Chase. After founding the Provincetown School of Art on Cape Cod, Massachusetts, Hawthorne decided to establish a winter art school in Bermuda in 1910. In landscapes such as *Early Morning, Bermuda*, Hawthorne laid out a generalized view of sand, sea, and sky that transcends specific location to render the totality of the idealized Bermuda experience. As in Turner's reductive *Bermuda*, Hawthorne applied modulated watercolor washes across open horizontal planes to construct an image that unites an Impressionist sense of color and light with classical balance and order. Hawthorne probably would have shared his wife's observation that, "The colors of the sound and the sea are indescribable – all the varying shades of emerald...cerulean and deep blues".[52] Of course, he went on to describe precisely that visual experience.

E. Ambrose Webster (1869–1935) was Hawthorne's professional rival in Provincetown, where Webster also directed a successful art school. However, unlike Hawthorne, who continued to look to Impressionism for inspiration, Webster trumpeted the radical experiments of the European avant-garde painters. In Paris, he studied the geometric restructuring of reality with the Cubist Albert Gleizes, and he saw color transformed in Fauve painting. Perhaps at Anshutz's suggestion, Webster visited Bermuda in 1912 and returned several times thereafter. The flattened planes and grid-like composition of his Bermuda oil paintings, particularly *Cactus* (no. 7) and *Blue Aloe*, clearly demonstrate his commitment to the classical geometry of the Cubists, while the balance of complementary colors indicates Fauve influence.

Declaring Webster to be "a luminarist of the most modern order," a contemporary critic writing in the *Boston Evening Transcript* saw in his work the synthesis of a stylistic legacy with the immediate experience of Bermuda. The critic explained, "Not only the light but the heart and color of the tropics are strikingly felt in his canvases."[53] The Bermuda experience determined Webster's approach to composition and color in these paintings. A radically reduced structure of flattened shapes serves as a foil for the drama of light and shade rendered primarily through the juxtaposition of yellow and purple. "Several persons have asked me why, or then when, I became so sure shadows in the sunlight are purple," Webster explained in a 1919 interview. "I always thought so, but was not positive until I went to Bermuda where I now go every winter."[54] His interest in the expressive possibilities of radically simplified form and color made him an early champion of American Modernists such as Marsden Hartley.

Webster and Hawthorne persuaded Houghton Cranford Smith (1887–1983) to come to Bermuda to recuperate from lead poisoning in 1912. He stayed with Hawthorne and other friends from Provincetown, and he painted with Webster. Initially under Hawthorne's influence, Smith used an Impressionist or Post-Impressionist approach, but later gravitated to the greater structural refinement of modernist Purism, which he studied firsthand with Le Corbusier in the early 1930s. In *Après le Cubisme* (After Cubism), published in 1918, Le Corbusier and Amédée Ozenfant, presented Purism as a simplified, more mechanistic sequel to Cubism. Their own paintings of still life subjects were organized, as Gail Stavitsky explains, according to "strict, rational laws of composition and form to convey a new world order".[55] Smith's oil paintings, *Bermuda Houses by Water* and *House with Red Amaryllis, Bermuda*, testify to his transition from Impressionist diffusion to the Purist call for "a return to the eternal, classical principles of structure and form...."[56] In the aftermath of World War I and during the frenetic years of the 1920s, many artists found this call to order appealing.



Just as painters had traveled from the United States to Bermuda for artistic or therapeutic reasons, artists from Canada also began to see the island as a site of renewal and inspiration. John Lyman (1886–1960), founder of the Contemporary Arts Society in Canada, first visited Bermuda in 1912 before going to Paris in 1913. He returned to the island the following year and various winters afterward. The island offered a refuge when his art was heavily criticized in Montreal and his marriage to a French-Canadian Catholic was condemned in the city's social circles.[57] The resulting strain caused Lyman's eyesight to deteriorate, and the steely skies, dark ultramarine water, and eerie foreground light of his painting, *St. George's, Bermuda* (no. 8) may reflect his physical and emotional difficulties. Yet, in spite of the strong contrast of light and dark in this work, the clearly defined geometric shapes create an armature of balanced horizontals and verticals and a profoundly still atmosphere that reflects the tranquility Lyman found in Bermuda.

Jack Bush (1909–1977) became Canada's leading abstract painter, and his Bermuda paintings combine his formal sensibility with vivid realism to convey the character of the island. *House and Figure, St. George's* (no. 9) depicts West Indians who landed in Bermuda on their way north aboard banana boats that plied the waters between the islands and U.S. ports. While Bush captures the essence of the West Indian figures and the solidity of the Bermuda architecture, he also transforms the image into a play of powerful contrasts of color and pattern. The foreground figure in primary red, blue, and yellow is set against the modulated whites of the house, which, in turn, stands brightly lit against an azure blue sky. The feather-like palm fronds are lively counterpoints to the strong geometry of the house. Bush and his wife came to Bermuda for their honeymoon in 1934, a period that marked the culmination of three decades during which prominent American Modernists had been discovering the island.



Traveling to Bermuda was an outgrowth of the relationships established among young American artists who, in the first and second decades of the twentieth century, were looking to the radical precedents of Cezanne, Matisse, and Picasso as guides to new ways of constructing visual experience. Painters such as Hartley, Charles Demuth, and Georgia O'Keeffe gathered around the photographer and art impresario Alfred Stieglitz. At his Gallery of the Photo-Secession, called "291" for its address on Fifth Avenue, Stieglitz exhibited the work of these new artists who became members of his circle. To encourage the exploration of new avenues of visual expression, he also presented exhibitions of recent European developments along with works from tribal Africa and Oceania. Inspired by the possibilities for abstraction these works suggested, members of the Stieglitz circle traveled to the Maine coast, Nova Scotia, New Mexico, or other regions of dramatic landscape to find the "essence and stark beauty" of the juncture of land, sea, and sky.[58]

Demuth (1883–1935) and Hartley were also regulars at the home of Walter and Louise Arensberg, whose New York apartment was the scene of exchanges between American and French Modernists including the painters Marcel Duchamp, Francis Picabia, Albert Gleizes, and the poet William Carlos Williams.[59] It was probably there that in 1916 Demuth, Hartley, Gleizes, and Gleizes's painter friend, Louis Bouché, decided to journey to Bermuda. In his painting, *Les Bermudes, La Maison du Gouverneur* (no. 10), Gleizes (1881–1953), transposed to the island the Cubist vision that he had been championing since he and his compatriot, Jean Metzinger, published *Du Cubisme*, the definitive treatise on Cubism, in 1912. Gleizes did not have to leave the Hamilton Hotel, where he, Bouché, Demuth, and Hartley first stayed, to look toward the towers of Government House and find inspiration for the classicized and modernist landscape he wished to create. This watercolor painting, which served as the basis of several large oil paintings, advanced the drive to bring classical, geometric order to nature. The framing verticals of trees, the generalized arcs of foliage, and the cubic forms of buildings recall the seventeenth-century Claudian formula, here updated into a structure of flattened parallel planes moving simultaneously upward on the surface and deeper into space. The cool blue-green tonalities play off the warm toned paper with an airy liveliness that contrasts with the generally subdued coloration of Cubist paintings.

Demuth's trip to Bermuda in the winter of 1916 furthered his goals of defining a structural form-language for his art and establishing himself within the Modernist avant-garde. Born in Lancaster, Pennsylvania, his early education at Franklin and Marshall Academy led to a scientific certificate, and his training at the Drexel Institute in Philadelphia reinforced his developing interest in structure and order. Through Anshutz, one of his teachers at the Pennsylvania Academy of Fine Arts, Demuth began to make contact with other Modernists in Philadelphia, including the writers William Carlos Williams, Marianne Moore, and Ezra Pound. Two trips to Europe and study at a Paris academy also expanded his horizons. By the end of the first decade of the twentieth century, Demuth had achieved some recognition as a watercolorist and a Modernist.[60]

From 1912 to 1914, Demuth made his most important trip to Europe, during which he attended the Academies Julian, Moderne, and Colarossi, met Gertrude and Leo Stein, traveled to Berlin with Hartley, painted on the French coast at Etretat, and wrote a one-act play, *The Azure Adder*.[61] Returning to the United States shortly before war erupted in Europe, he spent the summer of 1914 in Provincetown, where he experimented with Cubist abstractions under the influence of the nautical motifs Hartley had been painting in Germany. Demuth also worked with the Provincetown Players, where he met Eugene O'Neill. Their continuing friendship is implied in the playwright's invention of Charlie Marsden, the leading character in O'Neill's play, *Strange Interlude*, who is almost certainly a composite of Charles Demuth and Marsden Hartley.[62] By the following fall, Demuth embarked on the most fruitful period of his career. He had met Duchamp, Picabia, and Gleizes at the Arensberg's salon, and he had simplified his style under the evolving influence of Purism, which the French artists advocated.[63] Excited by the possibilities of this new approach, Demuth joined Hartley, Gleizes and Bouché in Bermuda to discuss Cubism and other Modernist concepts.

Demuth's Bermuda watercolor paintings certainly testify to Gleizes's influence as he worked to clarify his vision of an ordered and avant-garde world. Abandoning his earlier more sinuous forms and brighter Fauve color, Demuth assimilated the Purist aesthetic in his *Architecture: Red Roof and Trees and Houses* (no. 11), in which houses become transparent cubes and prisms and tree trunks provide isolated serpentine elements in contrast to the clarity of the ruler-drawn grid.[64] Delicate translucent washes, which capture the pastel hues of Bermuda's vernacular architecture, shimmer against this structure. Using a blotting technique to make fine tonal gradations and mottled textures, Demuth allowed the paint to dissolve into the surface of the paper in order to create a play of space against the flatness of the shapes. Defying gravity even more than Gleizes's structures do, Demuth's buildings seem to float peacefully like a mirage suspended above the earth.

These paintings mark a watershed in Demuth's development and crystallize the style that would be called Precisionism. Demuth's Bermuda works served as a guide as Precisionism developed in America "within the international context of the classicizing, constructive machine age 'call to order' movements," that, Gail Stavitsky observes, "evolv[ed] after the chaos and destruction of World

War I."[65] Yet, in its clarity and order, as well as its response to the horrors of war, Precisionism also is linked to earlier American interpretations of landscape, particularly Luminism. Defining Demuth's approach as a "method almost scientific in its precision," the critic Forbes Watson extolled "its refinement, its reticence, its disdain of all that is heavy-handed" and concluded that Demuth was a quintessentially American Modernist "in tune with everything that has hitherto been finest in American art."[66] Along with Demuth, Niles Spencer (1893–1952) and George Ault (1891–1948) applied the Precisionist approach to their own experiences in Bermuda.

Ault visited the island in 1922, and the quiet beauty of the numerous monotypes, watercolors, and pencil drawings he created there suggest that he enjoyed a brief period of serenity in an otherwise unhappy life. In his watercolor, *A Street in St. George's* (no. 12), for example, he reduced the stucco walls of the vernacular architecture of the town to a play of clearly defined, flat, orange and violet planes that simultaneously recede toward a golden light. In his Bermuda landscapes, Ault added poetic color and light to the geometric structure and emotional reserve that typify Precisionism.

When he visited the island in 1927, Spencer saw Bermuda's vernacular architecture as part of its peaceful atmosphere. The clustered masses of houses that fill the space of Spencer's oil painting, *House, Bermuda (St. George's)* (no. 13), reduce the natural environment to a generalized mass of dark green foliage in the background. The houses manifest the human presence in Bermuda, and their simple geometry speaks of the harmony that Spencer observed. As with Cezanne, Spencer found geometry everywhere. The critic Henry McBride characterized him as "one of those who sees cubism in nature,"[67] and Spencer's art is also classical in spirit. "In esthetic and technique the context of Spencer's art is cubism," Holger Cahill noted, "but the personal quality, the dignity, the distance, and precision are those of the classic."[68] Spencer's and Ault's classical Precisionist rendering of Bermudan spaces and structures contrast with Georgia O'Keeffe's more organic and naturalistic response to the island.

Georgia O'Keeffe (1887–1986) came to Bermuda in March 1933 seeking refuge from the stress of her professional and personal life. The failure of her project to paint a mural in Radio City Music Hall and difficulties in her marriage to Alfred Stieglitz in late 1932 led to physical and emotional symptoms: constricted breathing, loss of appetite, inability to walk or sleep. After spending two months in treatment for "psycho-neurosis" at Doctor's Hospital in New York in February and March 1933, she left immediately for Bermuda. As she wrote to her friend Rebecca Strand, wife of the photographer Paul Strand, "a place where the sun shines and it is warm – where no one will ask me how I feel and no one I know will be around seems very good to think of."[69] The following month, she again wrote to Strand, "It is all curiously quiet and easy moving... the household like the weather... like the islands... it all seems a bit unreal." She observed much but could do no work. "It is warm and slow and the sea such a lovely clear greenish blue," she told Strand. "I have done little but sit – but the sitting is good."[70]

By May, she felt strong enough to return to New York, but in February 1934, the northern winter weather and loneliness brought her back to Bermuda. She stayed with friends in a house called the Parapet on Scaur Hill, Somerset, next door to the house Winslow Homer probably occupied thirty-three years earlier.[71] Bermuda is "warm and soft and lovely," she wrote to her friend Jean Toomer, "and there is no one about who connects at all with the New York life...and the ocean is in between." After an eighteen-month hiatus, she began to work again. "I've been drawing a little," she explained to Toomer. "It all seems much more beautiful than I thought it last year... I can lie here or sit... and look out at the water over the tops of cedar trees... all really very good."[72]

In this therapeutic atmosphere, O'Keeffe produced eleven drawings, including *Banyan Tree Trunk, Bermuda* (no. 21). This East Indian transplant to the island spreads branches like new shoots over large areas of the ground. However, O'Keeffe focused on the heart of the tree, where its massive branches spring from a complex core. She was more interested in the essence of the tree, which she defined in a few monumental cylindrical forms described with delicate pencil shading. These drawings have a dignity and austerity that would also inform O'Keeffe's later images of the New Mexican landscape.

Unlike his friends, Gleizes and Demuth, Marsden Hartley (1877–1943) did not travel to Bermuda in the winter of 1916 simply to get away from the generally hectic wartime environment of New York. For Hartley, the island offered the possibility of companionship and stability in a time of total emotional dislocation. Between 1910 and 1915, he had been productive and happy living in Europe, particularly in Germany where he met artists such as Wassily Kandinsky and Franz Marc and where his increasingly abstract paintings were received positively. However, by the winter of 1915, his friend Karl von Freiburg had been killed in battle, and food shortages forced him to leave Germany. "For all the suffering he had witnessed in Berlin," Barbara Haskell explains, "the city had given him the home and security he had always lacked. His forced withdrawal from this congenial atmosphere left him feeling psychologically orphaned.... Not only was he separated from his closest friends, but he now found himself in an environment where these very friends were regarded as the enemy."[73] In the polarized wartime atmosphere of New York City, even the music of Beethoven and Mozart was banned.

While Hartley struggled to find place for himself in his native land, his artist friends offered him the possibility of renewal. In the summer of 1916, the writer John Reed invited Hartley to join him in Provincetown. Reed's other guests included Leo Stein, William and Marguerite Zorach, Eugene O'Neill, Demuth, and Carl Sprinchorn, who would later become one of Hartley's closest friends. In the calm atmosphere of outer Cape Cod, Hartley abandoned the Expressionist symbolism of his German period and, under the influence of Synthetic Cubism, focused on the formal issues of compositions reduced to unified, geometric shapes in muted colors.[74] After Reed closed his house, Hartley and Demuth remained in Provincetown living in a rent-free house they found. The plan to go to Bermuda that winter offered Hartley an opportunity to prolong the pleasure of camaraderie and to continue his effort to refine his new reductive, formal approach. "I want my work in both writing and painting," he wrote to Sprinchorn in the winter of 1917, "to have that special coolness for I weary of emotional excitement in art...."[75] Under the influence of Demuth and Gleizes in Bermuda, Hartley's desire to find stability in retreat was manifested in spare still-life compositions of interior spaces.

For Hartley, the 1930s were in many ways a reprise of the events of 1916, as Europe moved steadily to repeat the history of World War I. He had returned to Europe in 1920 and had remained there until early 1934 when the financial crisis of the worldwide Depression forced him back to the United States. He joined the Public Works of Art Project grateful for the $55 weekly salary it offered. When that program was discontinued in May 1934 and his paintings were not sold, his always-precarious personal finances reached the crisis stage. Stieglitz, who had exhibited his work and had often advanced him money, declined to help, and a Guggenheim fellowship Hartley had received was not renewed. To add insult to injury, many friends rejected him because they viewed his stay in Germany as an indication of support for the National Socialist regime. "All I want is to live modestly without terror of hunger," he protested to his friend Louis Shapiro, "and I can go on and produce quietly...."[76] In this atmosphere of alienation and despair, Hartley destroyed the paintings he could no longer afford to store. Desperate to leave New York, he planned to escape to New England by summer, but his doctor forbade him to go north because persistent bronchitis was sapping his strength.

The idea of Bermuda as a place of salvation began to take shape in Hartley's mind. The sale of a painting to his nephew, Theodore Newell, as well as a monthly stipend of $50 from an "angel", made the prospect a reality. In June, he made the three-day voyage to the island where, as he explained in a letter to Rebecca Strand, he could live as one of "the elegant poor".[77] He took a room for $15 a month in the north shore home of Elmo Petty, a local plumber. On weekends, Petty went out to the coral reefs to fish. Hartley went along and discovered shoals of brilliantly colored sea creatures. His oil painting, *Sunken Treasure* (no. 14), is Hartley's record of this remarkable discovery. In this image, the fish and the coral in shimmering primary colors take on a magical presence that transcends specific time or place. The viewer simultaneously looks down into the water and at the creatures floating in space. Their simplified, flattened forms and decorative organization become emblematic of a place where the experience of nature is at once reassuring and transformative. Hartley had found in his sojourn in Bermuda the treasure that American artists had been seeking since Thomas Doughty sailed to Mount Desert Island – a projection in nature of his own hope for the elusive perfect world.

# ENDNOTES

1 Quoted in Patricia Calnan, *The Masterworks Bermudiana Collection* (Hamilton, Bermuda: The Bermudian Publishing Co. Ltd., 1994), p. 28.

2 Quoted in Kynaton McShine (ed.), "Toward the Abstract Sublime," in Kynaston McShine (ed.), *The Natural Paradise: Painting in America 1800–1950* (New York: Museum of Modern Art, 1976), p. 109.

3 John Wilmerding, *American Views: Essays on American Art* (Princeton, NJ: Princeton University Press, 1991), p. 85.

4 Nicolai Cikovsky, Jr., "American Landscape," in Marilyn S. Kushner, et al., *Three Hundred Years of Painting: The Montclair Art Museum Collection* (New York: Hudson Hills Press and the Montclair Art Museum, 1989), p. 27.

5 Wilmerding, *American Views*, p. 3.

6 Cikovsky, "American Landscape," p. 29.

7 Albert Boime, *The Magisterial Gaze: Manifest Destiny and American Landscape Painting* (Washington, DC and London: Smithsonian Institution Press, 1991), p. 5.

8 Ralph Waldo Emerson, "Nature" [1836] in *The Works of Ralph Waldo Emerson*, vol. II. Nature, Addresses and Lectures (Cambridge: Riverside Press, 1903–1904), pp. 7–8. Quoted in Susan Faxon, *Point of View: Landscapes from the Addison Collection* (Andover, MA: Addison Gallery of American Art, 1992), p. 9.

9 Barbara Novak, *Nature and Culture: American Landscape Painting 1825–1875* (New York and Oxford: Oxford University Press, 1995), p. 273.

10 Thomas Cole, "Essay on American Scenery" [1835], *The American Monthly Magazine*, New Series 1 (January 1836), p. 5. Quoted in Barbara Novak (editor and introduction), "On Divers Themes from Nature," in McShine, *The Natural Paradise*, pp. 61–62.

11 William Cullen Bryant, *Poetical Works* (New York: D. Appleton and Company, 1897), p. 64.

12 Thomas Cole, letter to Luman Reed, March 6, 1836 (Cole Papers). Quoted in Oswaldo Rodriguez Roque, "The Exaltation of American Landscape Painting," in John K. Howat, et al., *American Paradise: The World of the Hudson River School* (New York: Metropolitan Museum of Art and Harry Abrams, 1987), p. 128.

13 Thomas Cole, *Thomas Cole's Poetry*. Edited by Marshall B. Tynn (York, PA: Liberty Cap Books, 1972), p. 103. Quoted in Novak, *Nature and Culture*, p. 157.

14 Faxon, *Point of View*, p. 29.

15 Jasper Cropsey, "Up among the Clouds," *The Crayon* (New York) vol. 2, no. 6 (August 8, 1855), p. 79. Quoted in Novak in McShine, *The Natural Paradise*, p. 89.

[16] Asher B. Durand, "Letters," *The Crayon* (New York) vol. 1, no. 10 (January 3, 1855), p. 2. Quoted in Cikovsky, "American Landscapes," p. 32.

[17] Barbara Ball Buff, catalogue note, in Howat, *American Paradise,* p. 143.

[18] Unidentified newspaper clipping. Quoted in Rebecca Bedell, *The Anatomy of Nature: Geology and American Landscape Painting, 1825–1875* (Princeton, NJ: Princeton University Press, 2001), p. 87.

[19] Carol Tryon, catalogue note, in Howat, *American Paradise,* pp. 149–150.

[20] Henry David Thoreau, entry, December 15, 1838, *Journal of Henry D. Thoreau.* Edited by Carl Bode (New York: Signet, 1967), p. 34. Quoted in Novak, *Nature and Culture,* p. 150.

[21] "Domestic Art Gossip," *The Crayon* (New York) vol. 7, no. 12 (December 1860), p. 353. Quoted in Pamela J. Belanger, *Inventing Arcadia: Artists and Tourists at Mount Desert* (Rockland, ME: Farnsworth Art Museum, 1999), p. 98.

[22] Faxon, *Point of View,* p. 20.

[23] See Novak, *Nature and Culture,* p. 28.

[24] Belanger, *Inventing Arcadia,* p. 101.

[25] Sanford Gifford, 1877. Quoted in Nicolai Cikovsky, *Sanford Robinson Gifford, 1823–1880* (Austin: University of Texas Art Museum, 1970), p. 16.

[26] Samuel Clemens, *The Adventures of Huckleberry Finn* [1884] (New York: Crown Publishers, 1981), p. 96.

[27] John Wilmerding, "The Luminist Movement: Some Reflections," in John Wilmerding et al., *American Light: The Luminist Movement 1850–1875* (Washington, DC and New York: National Gallery of Art and Harper & Row, 1980), p. 146.

[28] *The Sign of Promise* [1863]. Quoted in Cikovsky, "American Landscapes," p. 34. See also Gail Stavitsky, "Introduction," in Gail Stavitsky et al., *George Inness: Presence of the Unseen* (Montclair, NJ: Montclair Art Museum, 1994), p. 9.

[29] Henry Ward Beecher, "Hours of Exaltation," (1857). Quoted in Peter Bermingham, *American Art in the Barbizon Mood* (Washington, DC: National Collection of Fine Arts, 1975), p. 29.

[30] Bermingham, *American Art,* p. 48.

[31] George Inness Jr., *Life, Art, and Letters of George Inness* [1917] (New York: DaCapo Press, 1969), p. 218.

[32] George Inness, *Exaltation,* in George Inness Jr., *Life, Art, and Letters,* p. 97.

[33] Linda Merrill, *An Ideal Country: Paintings by Dwight William Tryon in the Freer Gallery of Art* (Washington, DC: Freer Gallery of Art, 1990), p. 31.

[34] E.L. Godkin, editorial comment, *The Nation* (1866). Quoted in Samuel P. Hays, *Response to Industrialism: 1885–1914* (Chicago: University of Chicago Press, 1957), p. 25.

[35] Hays, *Response to Industrialism,* p. 24.

[36] Hays, *Response to Industrialism,* pp. 41–42. *Looking Backward* was the most widely read Utopian novel, selling 400,000 copies. It argued that humanity was inherently good and peaceful, not competitive and greedy, and that the environment could thwart or nurture noble instincts.

[37] John La Farge, *An Artist's Letters from Japan* (New York: Century, 1897), p. 1.

[38] La Farge, *An Artist's Letters,* pp. 88–89.

[39] H. Barbara Weinberg, Doreen Bolger, David Park Curry, *American Impressionism and Realism: The Painting of Modern Life, 1885–1915* (New York: Metropolitan Museum of Art and Harry Abrams, Inc., 1994), p. 92.

[40] Calnan, *Masterworks,* p. 13.

[41] Calnan, *Masterworks,* p. 13.

[42] Quoted in Calnan, *Masterworks,* p. 14.

[43] Helen A. Cooper, *Winslow Homer Watercolors* (Washington, DC and New Haven, CT: National Gallery of Art and Yale University Press, 1986), pp. 13–14.

[44] Quoted in Calnan, *Masterworks,* p. 13.

[45] Donelson F. Hoopes, *Winslow Homer Watercolors* (New York: Watson – Guptill Publishers, 1969), pp. 56–57.

[46] John Wilmerding, "Winslow Homer's Maine," in *American Views,* p. 44.

[47] Cooper, *Winslow Homer Watercolors,* p. 218.

[48] Wilmerding, "Winslow Homer's Maine," p. 39.

[49] Winslow Homer, letter to O'Brien and Son, Chicago, 1902 (Goodrich / Whitney Museum Record). Quoted in Cooper, *Winslow Homer Watercolors,* p. 226.

[50] Quoted in Hoopes, *Winslow Homer Watercolors,* p. 62.

[51] Calnan, *Masterworks,* p. 36.

[52] Mrs. Hawthorne, diary entry, 1910. Quoted in Calnan, *Masterworks,* p. 39.

[53] "Four Boston Painters," *Boston Evening Transcript,* January 8, 1913. Quoted in *The Next Decade: The Masterworks Bermudiana Collection* (Hamilton, Bermuda: The Bermuda National Gallery, 1997), p. 17.

[54] E. Ambrose Webster, interview, *Detroit Sunday News,* November 2, 1919. Quoted in *From Bermuda Palms to Northern Pines: Two Centuries of Art Inspired by Bermuda* (Toronto: University of Toronto Art Center, 2001), p. 8.

[55] Gail Stavitsky, 'Reordering Reality: Precisionist Directions in American Art, 1915–1941," in *Precisionism in America 1915–1941: Reordering Reality* (Montclair, NJ: Harry N. Abrams and the Montclair Art Museum, 1995), p. 15.

[56] Stavitsky, "Reordering Reality," p. 15.

[57] *From Bermuda Palms to Northern Pines, p. 3*

[58] Faxon, *Point of View,* p. 92.

[59] Stavitsky, "Reordering Reality," p. 12.

[60] Alvard L. Eiseman, *Charles Demuth* (New York: Watson-Guptil Publications, 1982), pp. 6–7.

[61] Eiseman, *Charles Demuth,* pp. 6–7.

[62] Calnan, *Masterworks,* p. 26. O'Neill may have joined Demuth and Hartley in Bermuda in 1916, and ten years later he purchased a large eighteenth-century house on the island's Harbour Road.

[63] Eiseman, *Charles Demuth,* p. 13.

[64] See Barbara Haskell, *Charles Demuth* (New York: Harry Abrams, 1988), pp. 121–141.

[65] Stavitsky, "Reordering Reality," p. 15.

[66] Forbes Watson, "American Note in Demuth's Art," *The World,* December 2, 1923, p. 8. Quoted in Stavitsky, "Reordering Reality," p. 18.

[67] Henry McBride, "Joseph Stella's Startling Art," *The Sun,* April 11, 1925, p. 9. Quoted in Stavitsky, "Reordering Reality," pp. 18–19.

[68] Holger Cahill, "Niles Spencer," *Magazine of Art,* vol. 45, November 1952. Quoted in Stavitsky, "Reordering Reality," p. 32.

[69] Georgia O'Keeffe, letter to Rebecca Strand, March 1933. Collection of American Literature, Beinecke Rare Book and Manuscript Library, Yale University. Quoted in *Georgia O'Keeffe – The Bermuda Respite* (Hamilton, Bermuda: The Masterworks Foundation, 1994), p. 13.

[70] Georgia O'Keeffe, letter to Rebecca Strand, April 1933. Collection of American Literature, Beinecke Rare Book and Manuscript Library, Yale University. Quoted in Calnan, *Masterworks,* p. 41.

[71] Calnan, *Masterworks,* p. 41.

[72] Georgia O'Keeffe, letter to Jean Toomer, 1934. Collection of American Literature, Beinecke Rare Book and Manuscript Library, Yale University. Quoted in *Georgia O'Keeffe – Bermuda Respite,* p. 19.

[73] Barbara Haskell, *Marsden Hartley* (New York: Whitney Museum of American Art and New York University Press, 1980), p. 52.

[74] Haskell, *Marsden Hartley,* pp. 54–55.

[75] Marsden Hartley, letter to Carl Sprinchorn, winter 1917, Archives of American Art. Quoted in Haskell, *Marsden Hartley,* p. 56.

[76] Marsden Hartley, letter to Louis Shapiro, January 2, 1935, Archives of American Art. Quoted in Haskell, *Marsden Hartley,* p. 97.

[77] Marsden Hartley, letter to Rebecca Strand, July 29, 1935, Archives of American Art. Quoted in Haskell, *Marsden Hartley,* pp. 97–98.

## PLATES



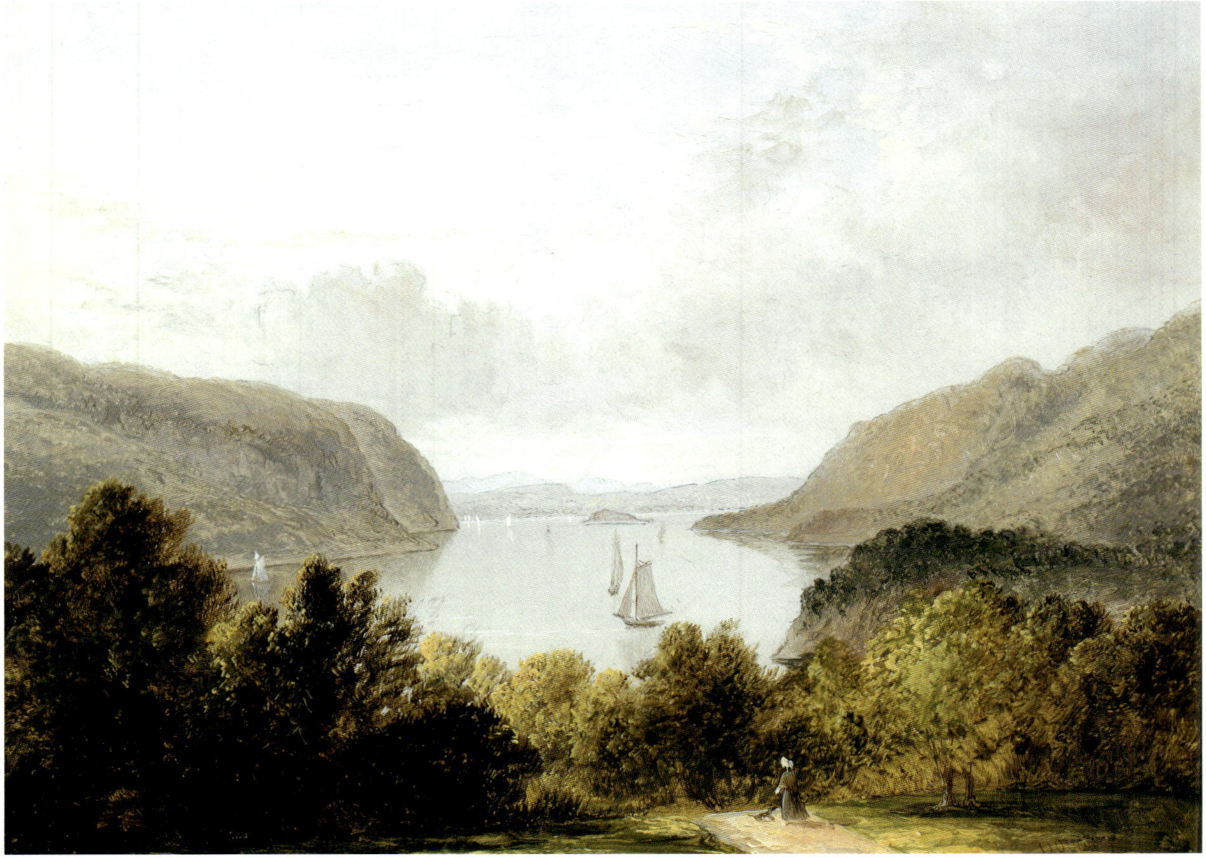

**No. 1**
Thomas Doughty (1793–1856)
*Hudson River near West Point*, c. 1835
Oil on board, 8.5 x 11.875 in.
The Montclair Art Museum, 1959.2
Gift of Mr. and Mrs. John C. Cattus

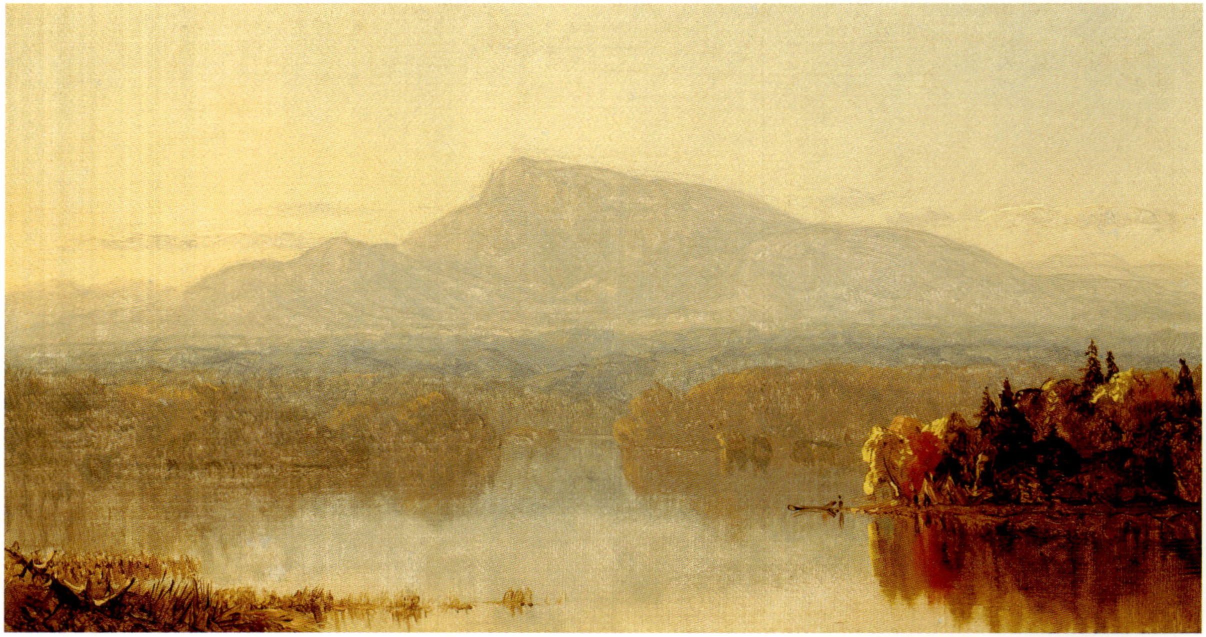

**No. 2**
Sanford Gifford (1823–1880)
*Lake Scene—Mountain Background,* 1867
Oil on canvas, 5.75 x 10.375 in.
Addison Gallery of American Art, Phillips Academy, Andover, Massachusetts
Bequest of Candace C. Stimson

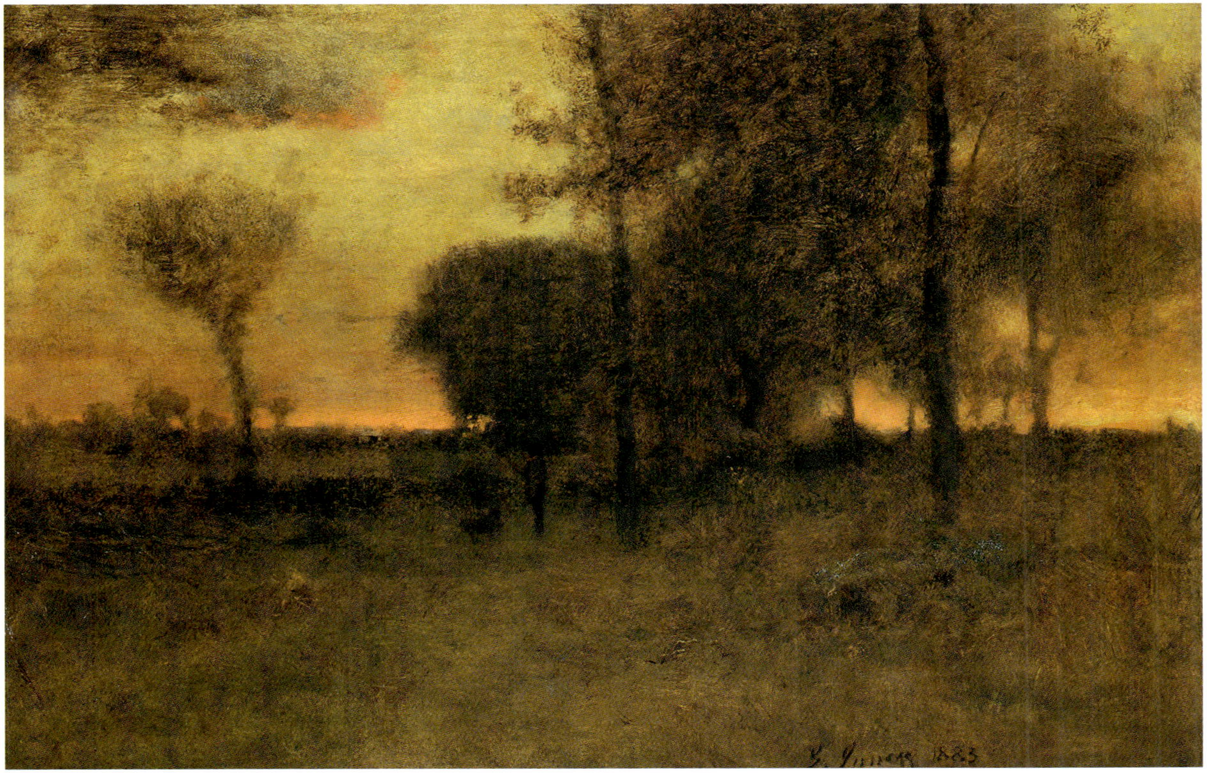

**No. 3**
George Inness (1825–1894)
*Sunset Glow*, 1883
Oil on paper mounted on board, 16 x 24.125 in.
The Montclair Art Museum, 1946.1
Gift of Francis M. Weld

**No. 4**
F. Childe Hassam (1859–1935)
*Morning Calm, Appledore,* 1901
Oil on canvas, 26 x 24.125 in.
Addison Gallery of American Art, Phillips Academy
Andover, Massachusetts
Gift of anonymous donor

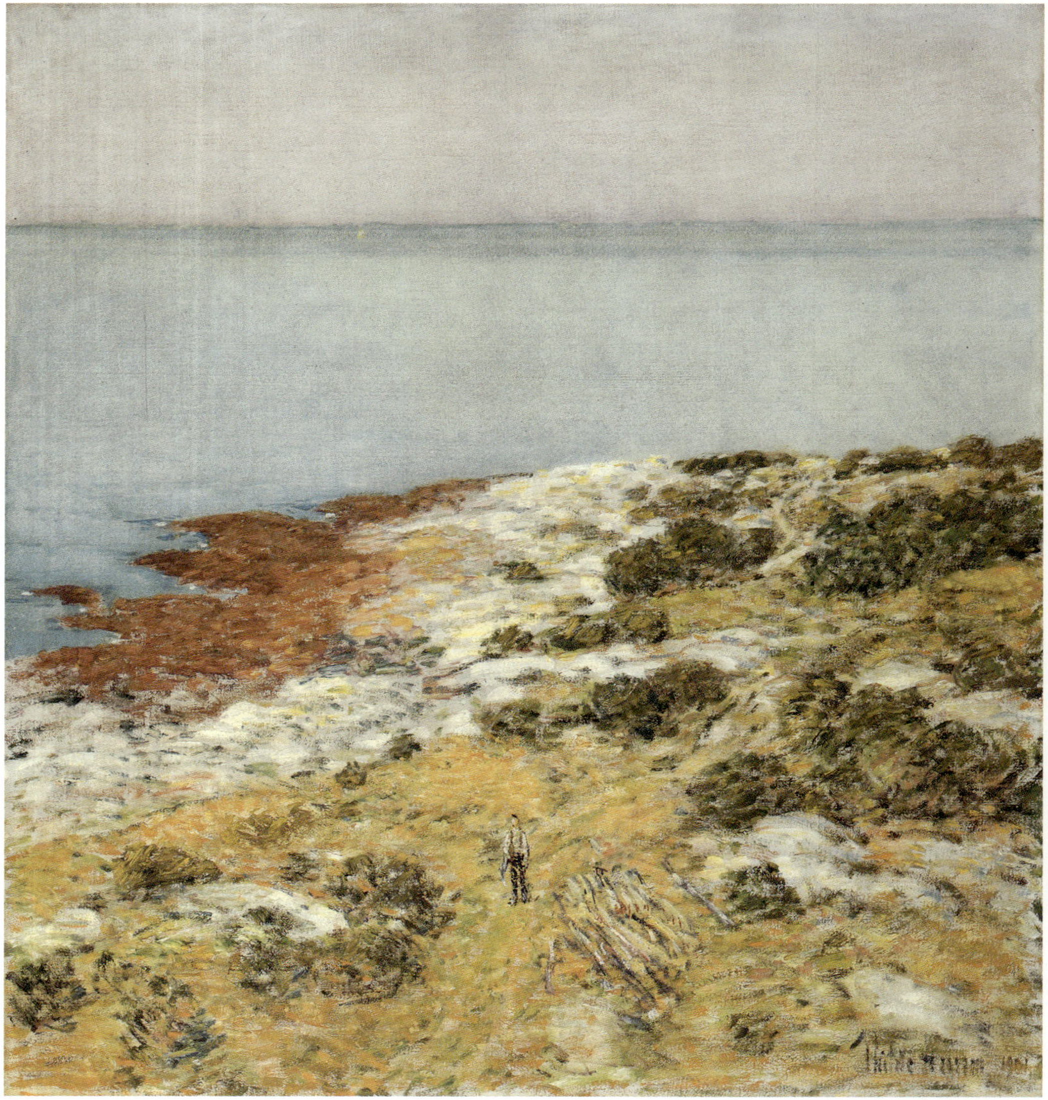

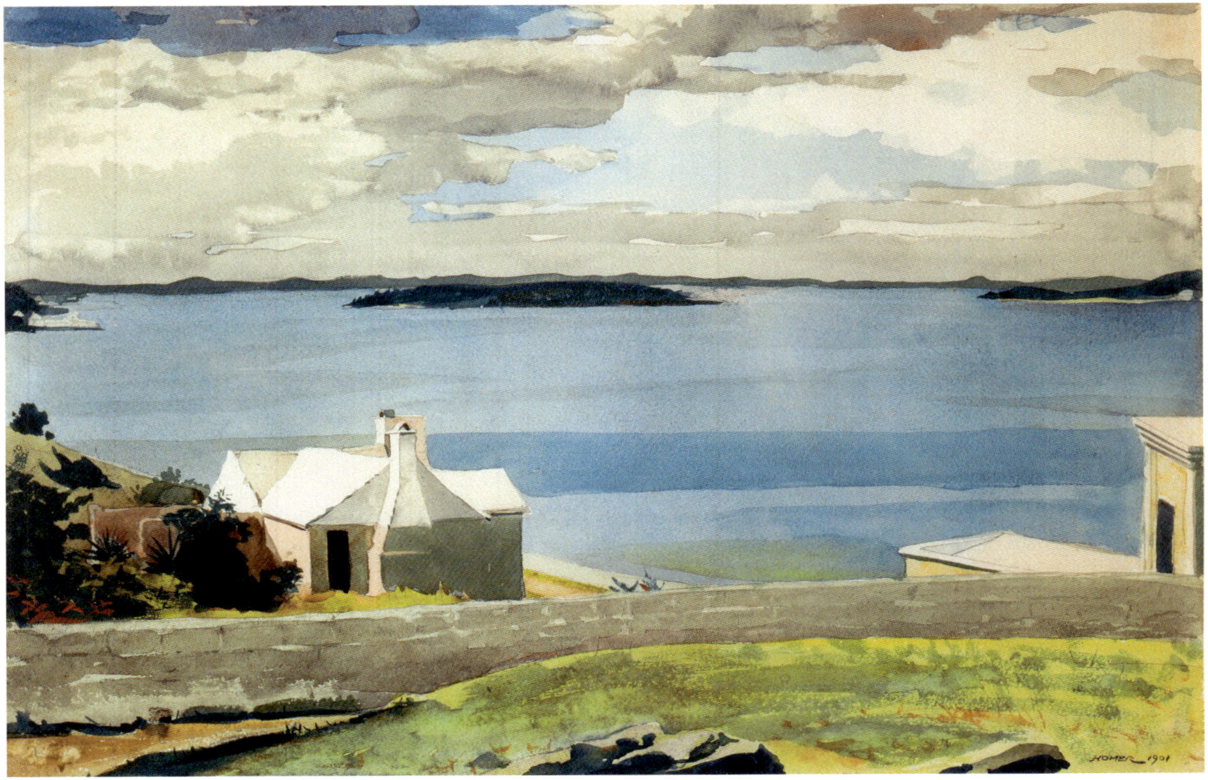




**No. 5**
Winslow Homer (1836–1910)
*Inland Waters*, 1901
Watercolor on paper,
13.75 x 21 in.
The Masterworks
Foundation, Bermuda

**No. 6**
Thomas Anshutz (1851–1912)
*View of Bermuda, South Shore,* 1911
Oil on canvas, 7.375 x 9.5 in.
The Masterworks Foundation, Bermuda

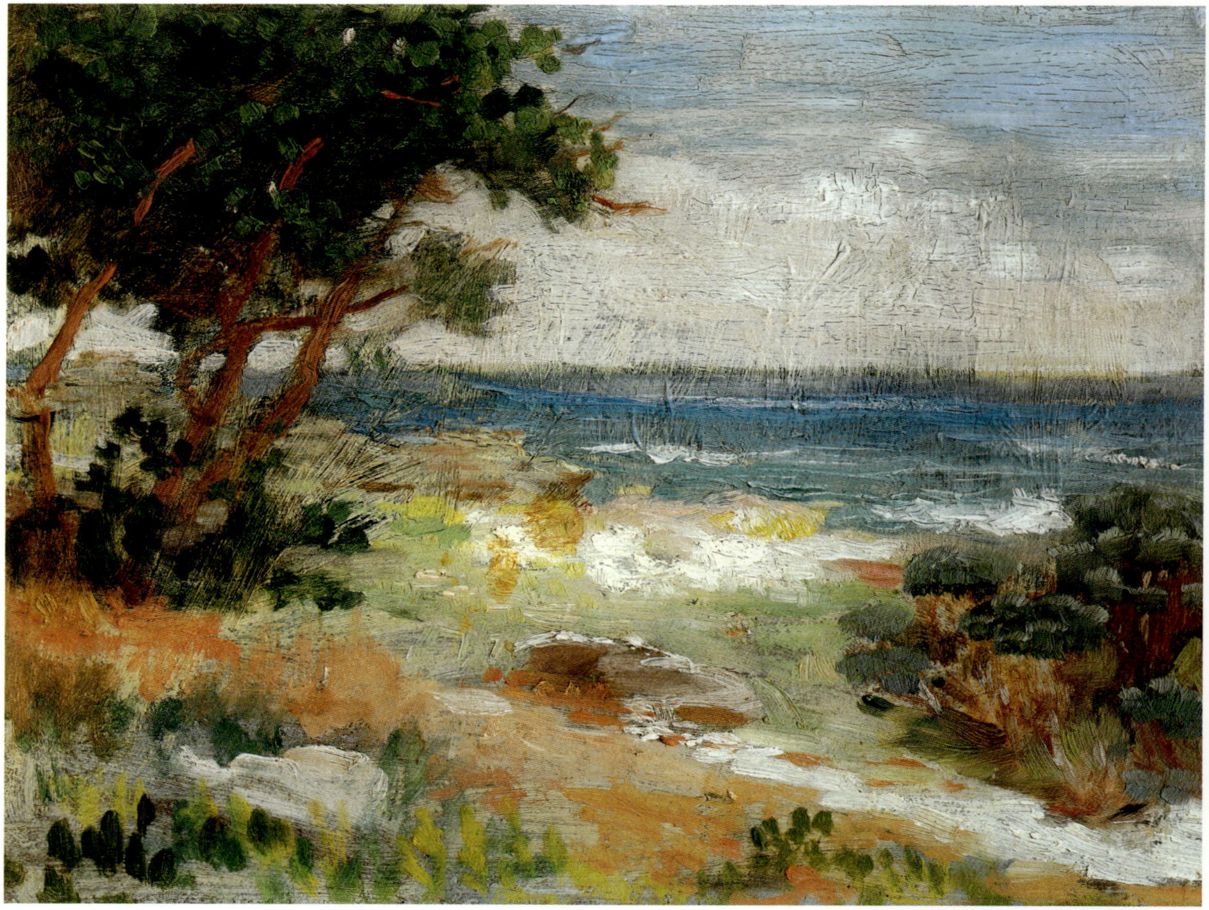

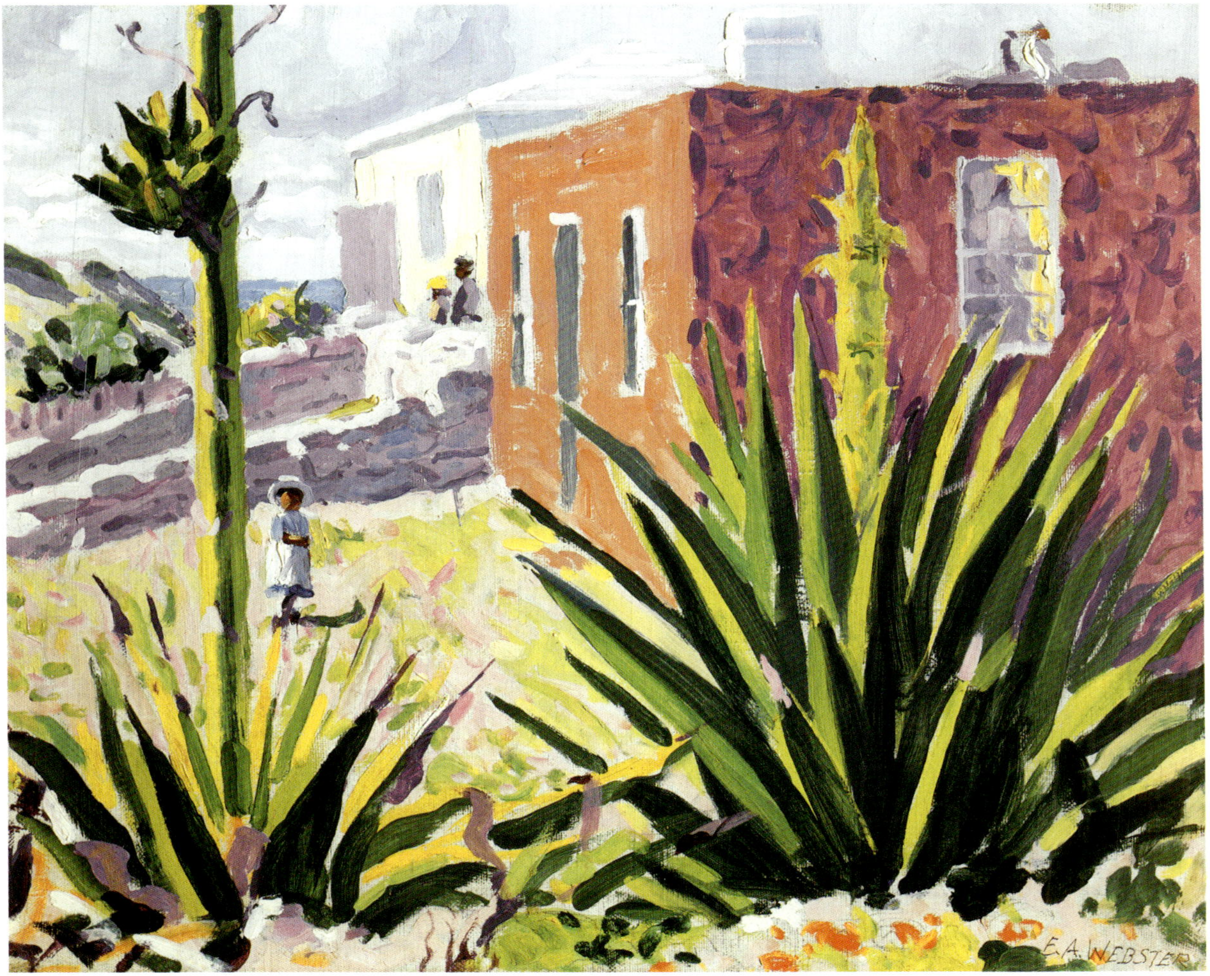




**No. 7**
E. Ambrose Webster
(1869–1935)
*Cactus*, 1915
Oil on canvas, 19.5 x 23.75 in.
The Masterworks
Foundation, Bermuda

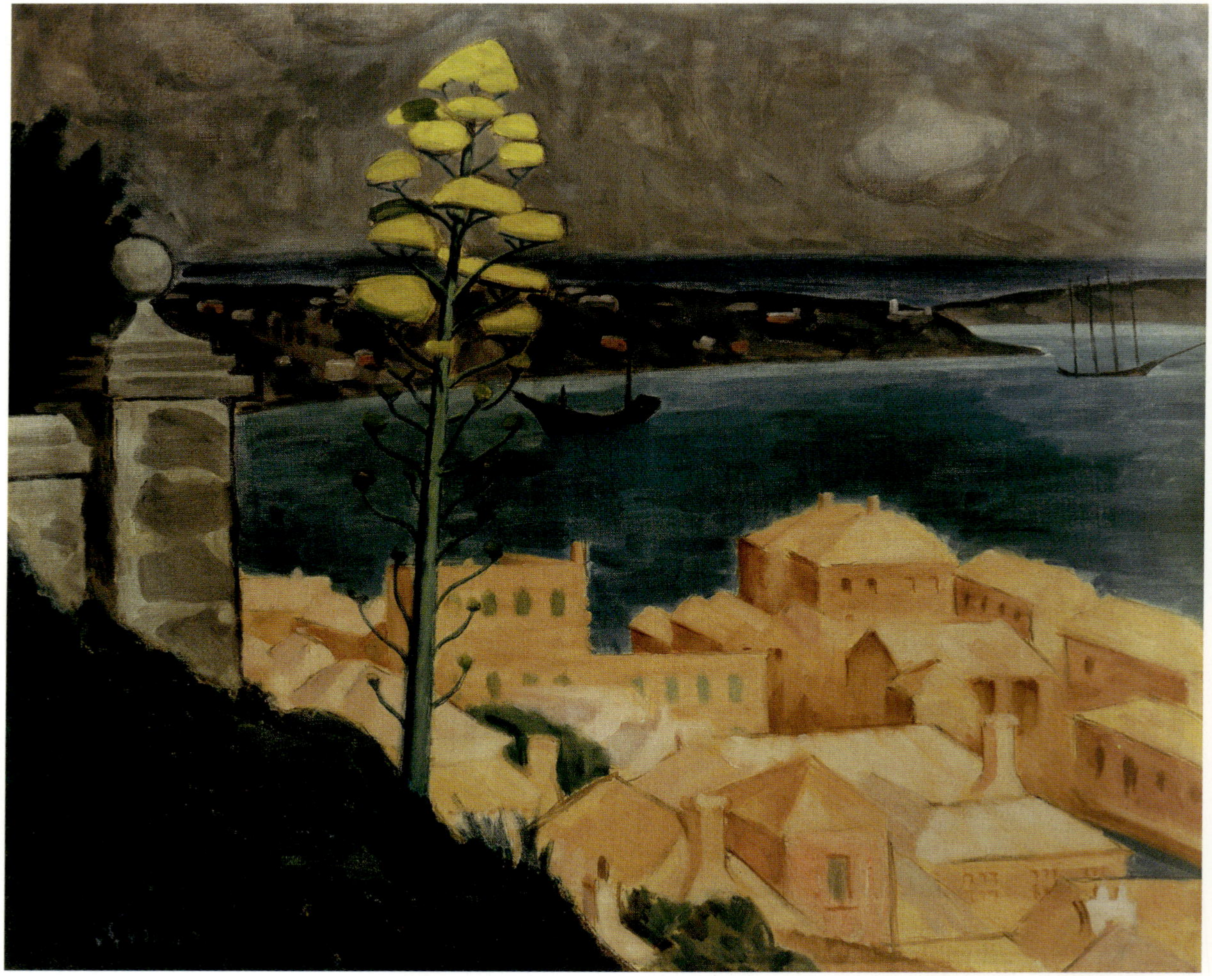

**No. 8**
John Lyman (1886–1960)
*St. George's, Bermuda*, c. 1920
Oil on canvas, 10.2 x 27.75 in.
The Masterworks
Foundation, Bermuda

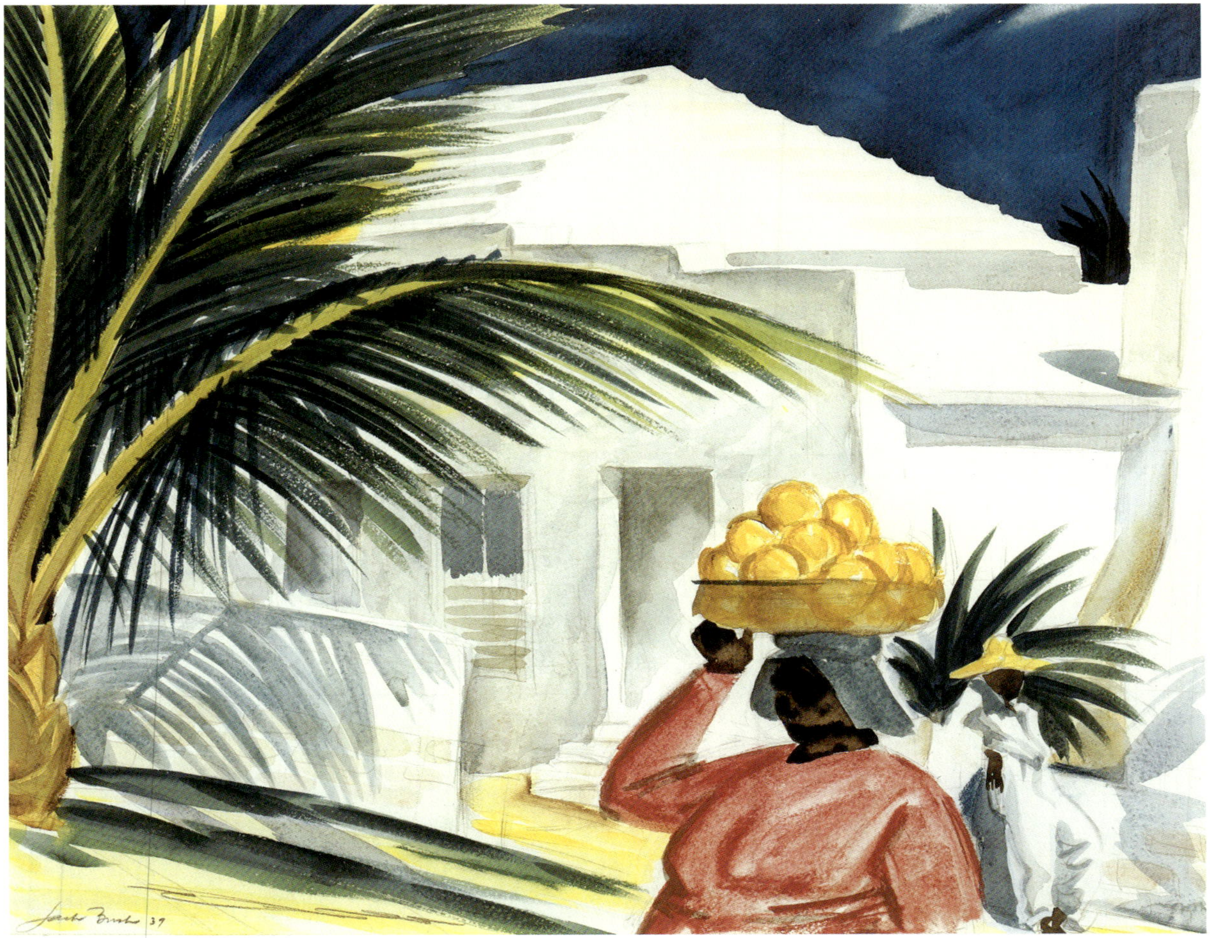

**No. 9**
Jack Bush (1909–1977)
*House and Figure, St. George's*, 1939
Watercolor and pencil on paper, 18.5 x 24 in.
The Masterworks Foundation, Bermuda

**No. 10**
Albert Gleizes (1881–1953)
*Les Bermudes, La Maison du Gouverneur*, 1917
Watercolor on paper,
10.25 x 8 in.
The Masterworks Foundation, Bermuda

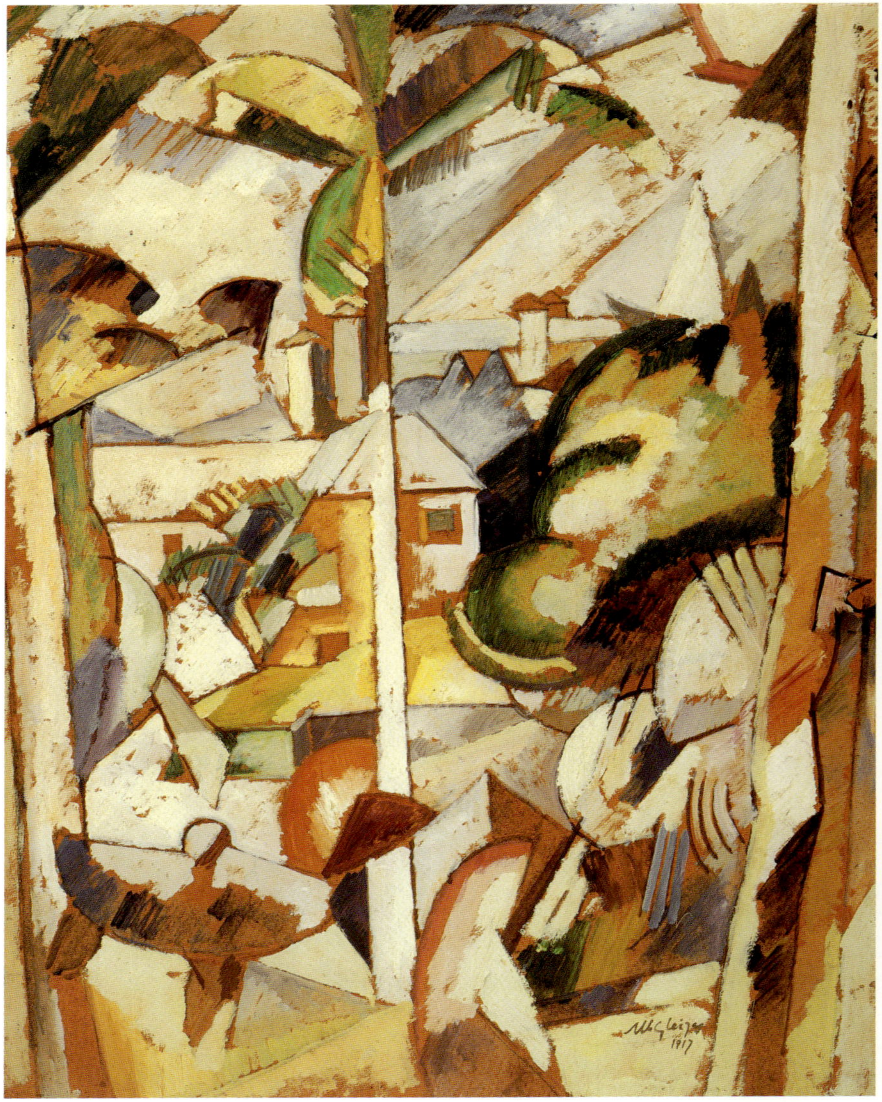

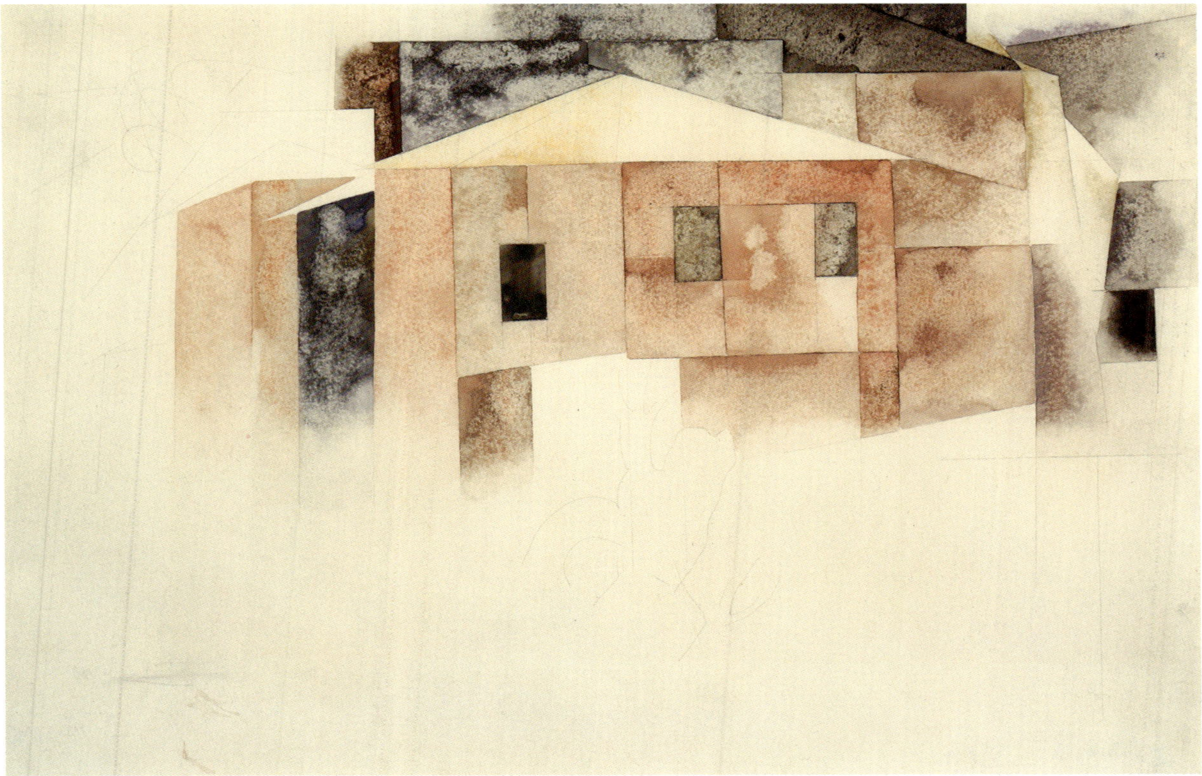



**No. 11**
Charles Demuth (1883–1935)
*Architecture: Red Roof,* 1917
Watercolor and pencil on paper, 11.75 x 17.75 in.
The Masterworks Foundation, Bermuda

**No. 12**
George Ault (1891–1948)
*A Street in St. George's*, 1922
Watercolor and pencil on
paper, 15 x 16.75 in.
The Masterworks
Foundation, Bermuda



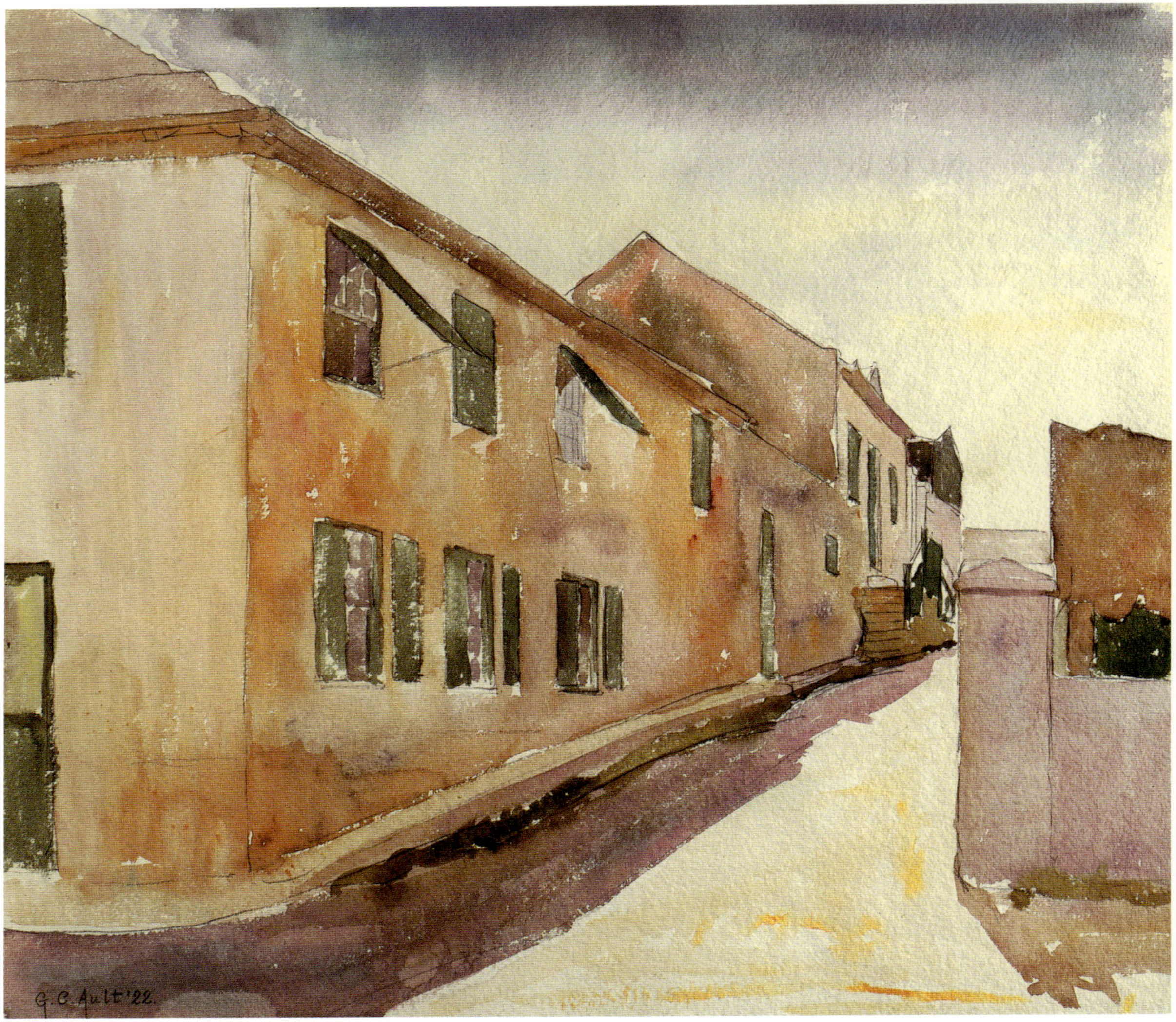

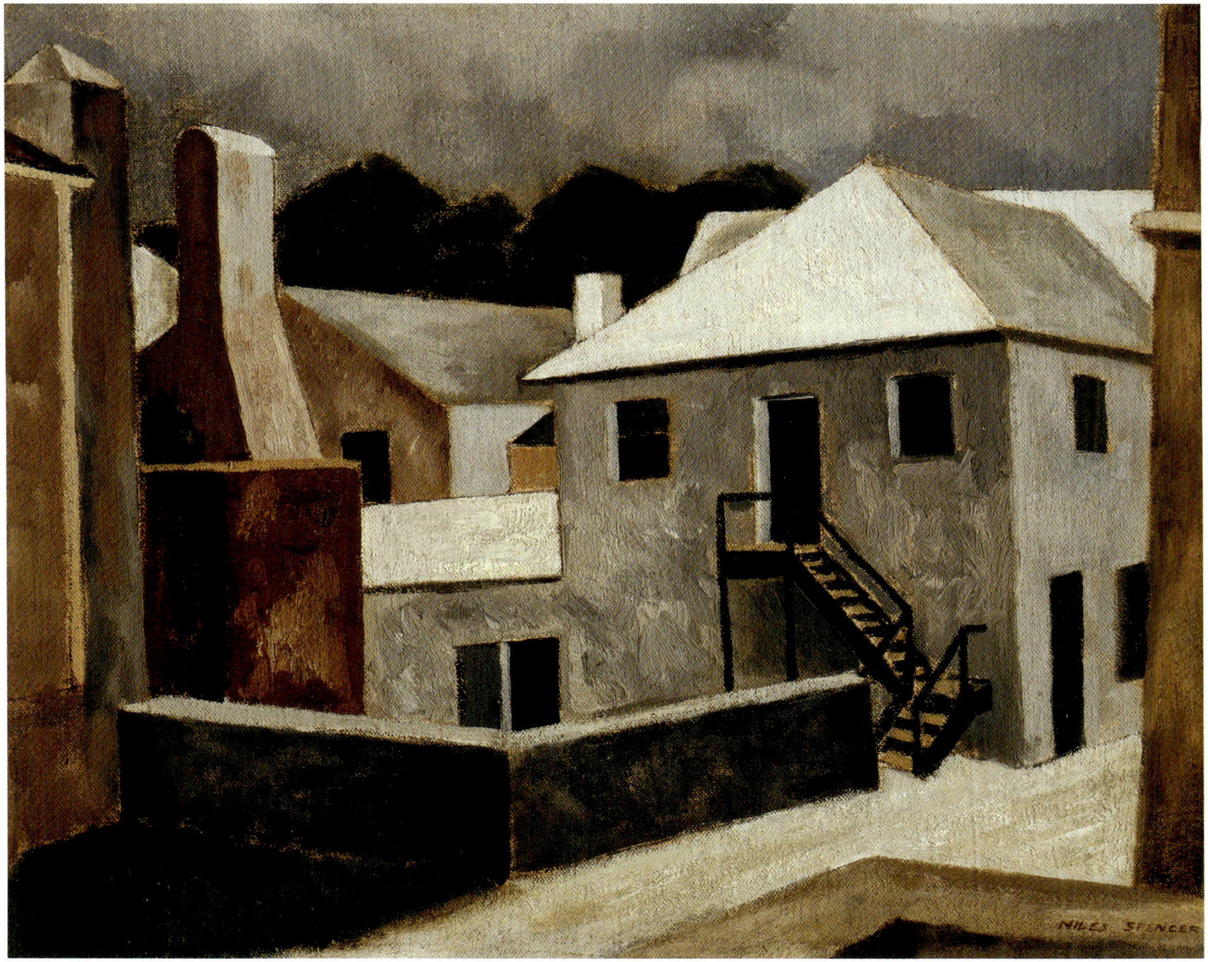


**No. 13**
Niles Spencer (1893–1952)
*House, Bermuda*
*(St. George's)*, 1929
Oil on board, 13 x 16 in.
The Masterworks
Foundation, Bermuda

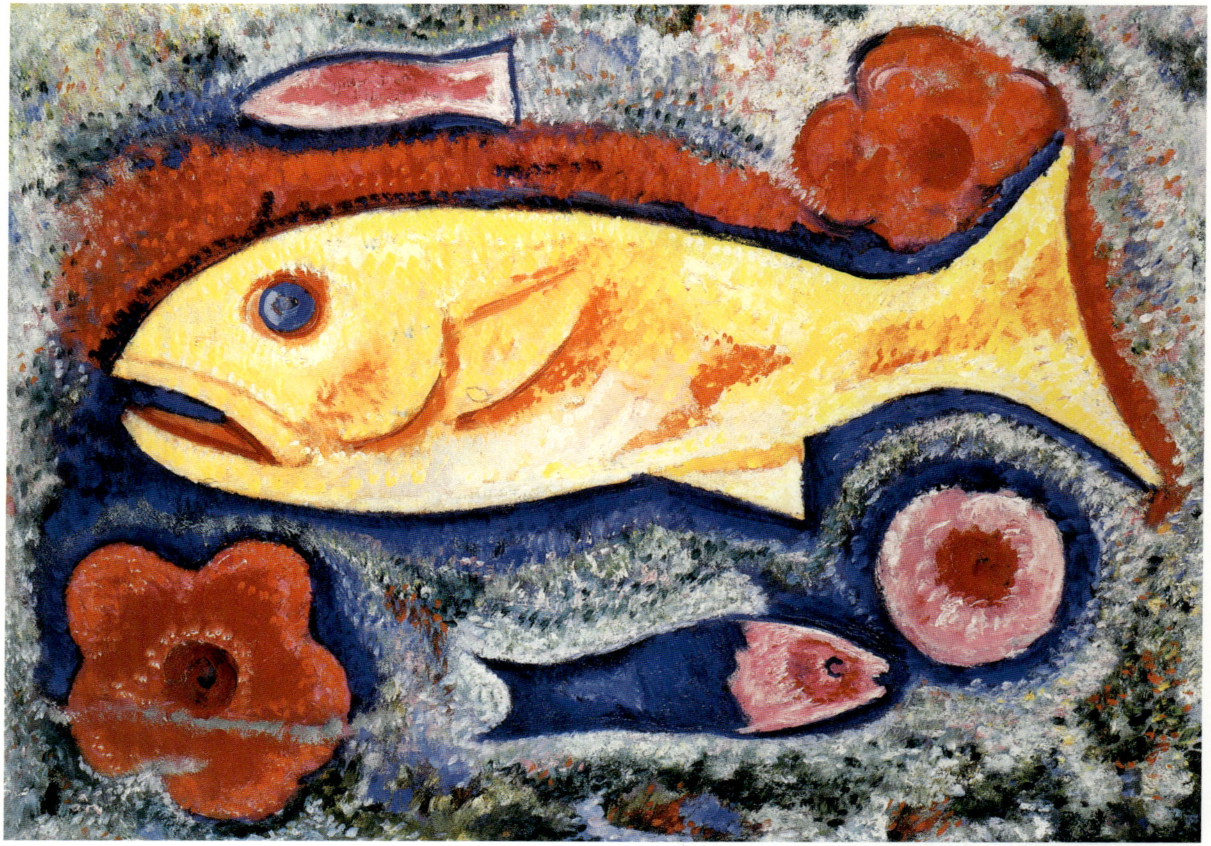

**No. 14**
Marsden Hartley (1877–1943)
*Sunken Treasure*, 1935
Oil on board, 18 x 24 in.
The Masterworks
Foundation, Bermuda

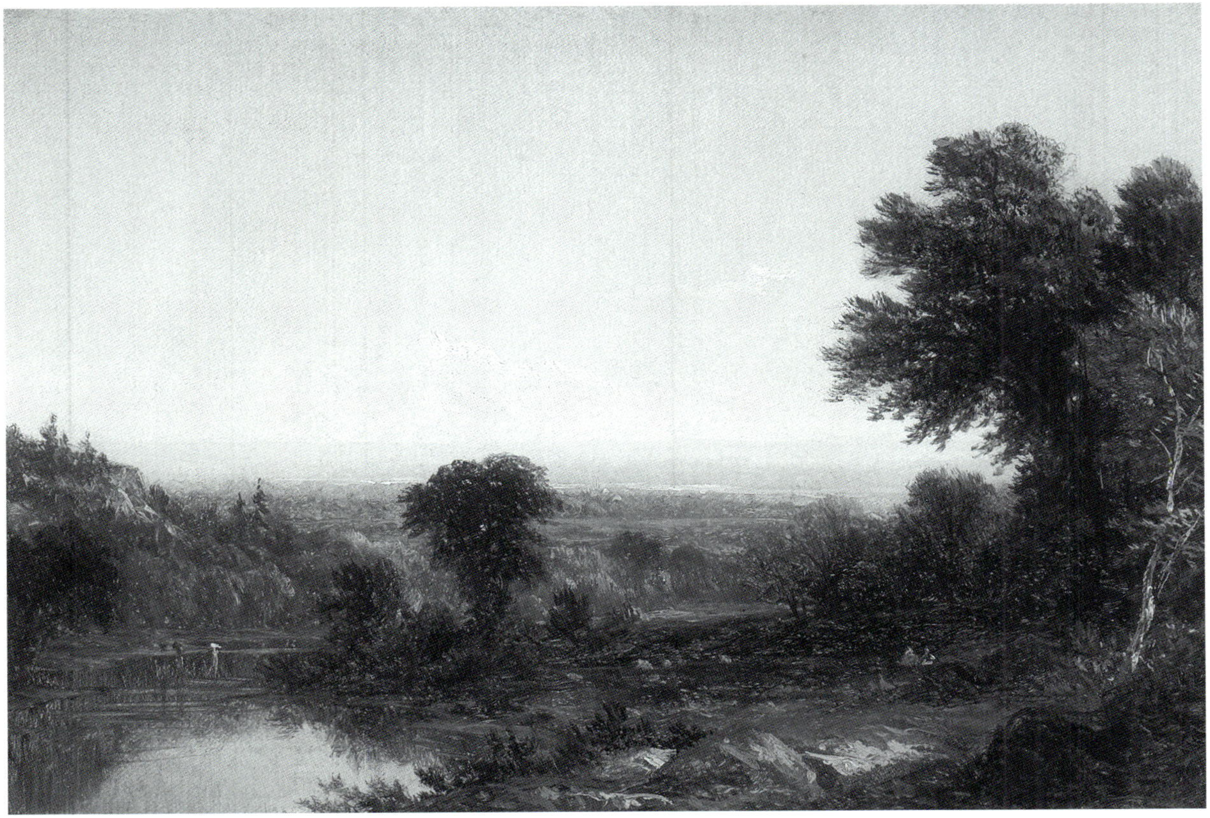

**No. 15**
John Casilear (1811–1893)
*Hudson River Scene*, c. 1850
Oil on board, 9 x 12.5 in.
Collection of Mr. and
Mrs. Alec H. Petro

**No. 16**
Benjamin Champney
(1817–1907)
*Mote Mountain from Walker's Pond*, 1878
Oil on canvas, 33 x 28 in.
Private Collection—
Boston College Alum

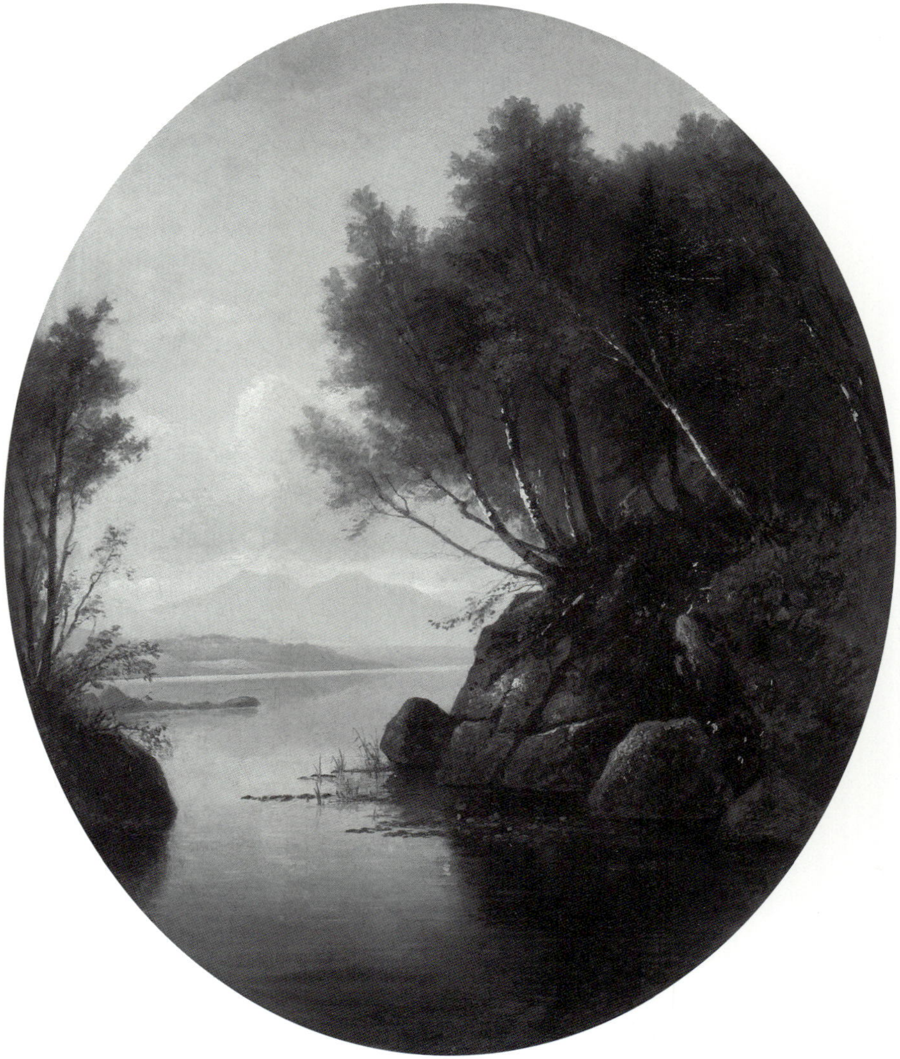

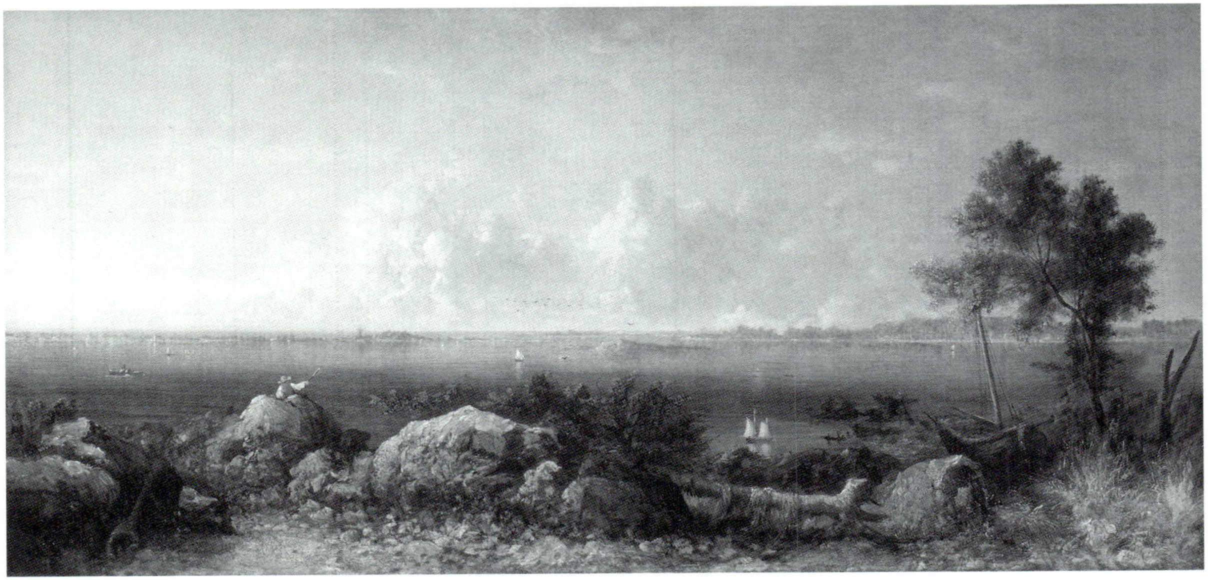

**No. 17**
George Loring Brown
(1814– 1889)
*View of Norwalk Islands, Norwalk, Connecticut*, 1864
Oil on canvas, 21.25 x 43.25 in.
Addison Gallery of American Art, Phillips Academy, Andover, Massachusetts

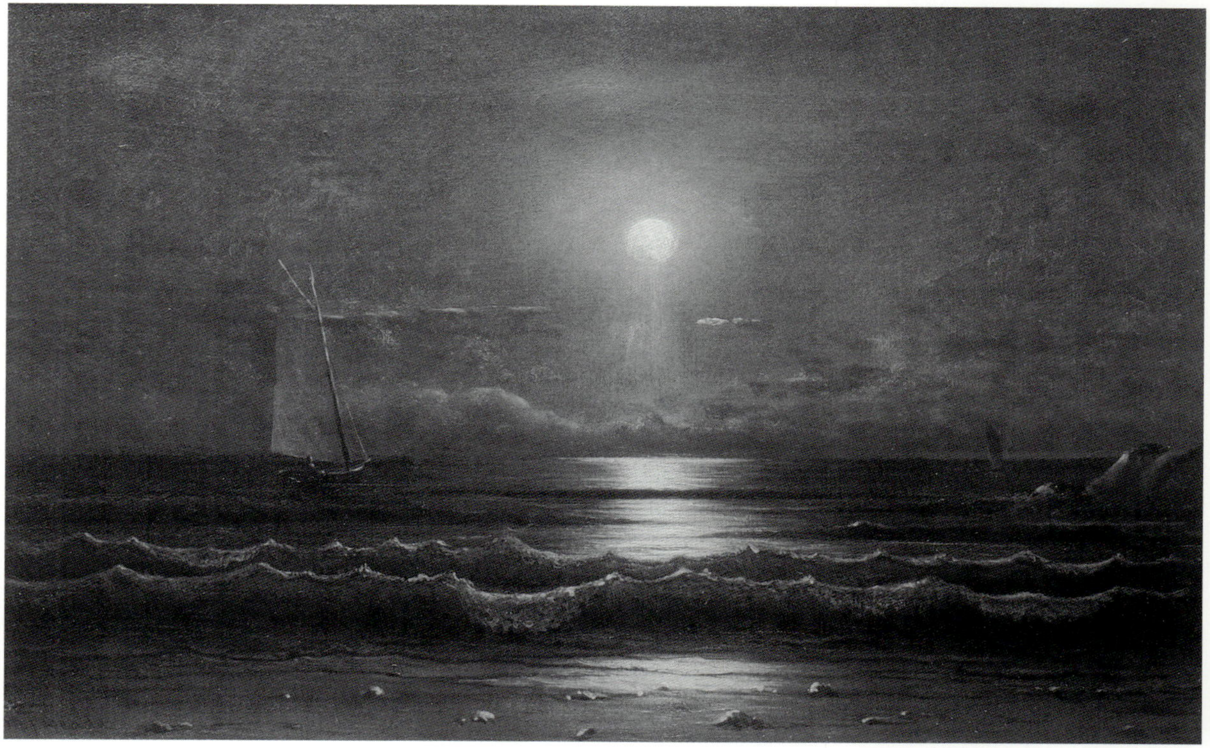

**No. 18**
Martin Johnson Heade
(1819–1904)
*Sailing by Moonlight*, c.
1870–1875
Oil on canvas, 14.25 x 22.25 in.
Private Collection

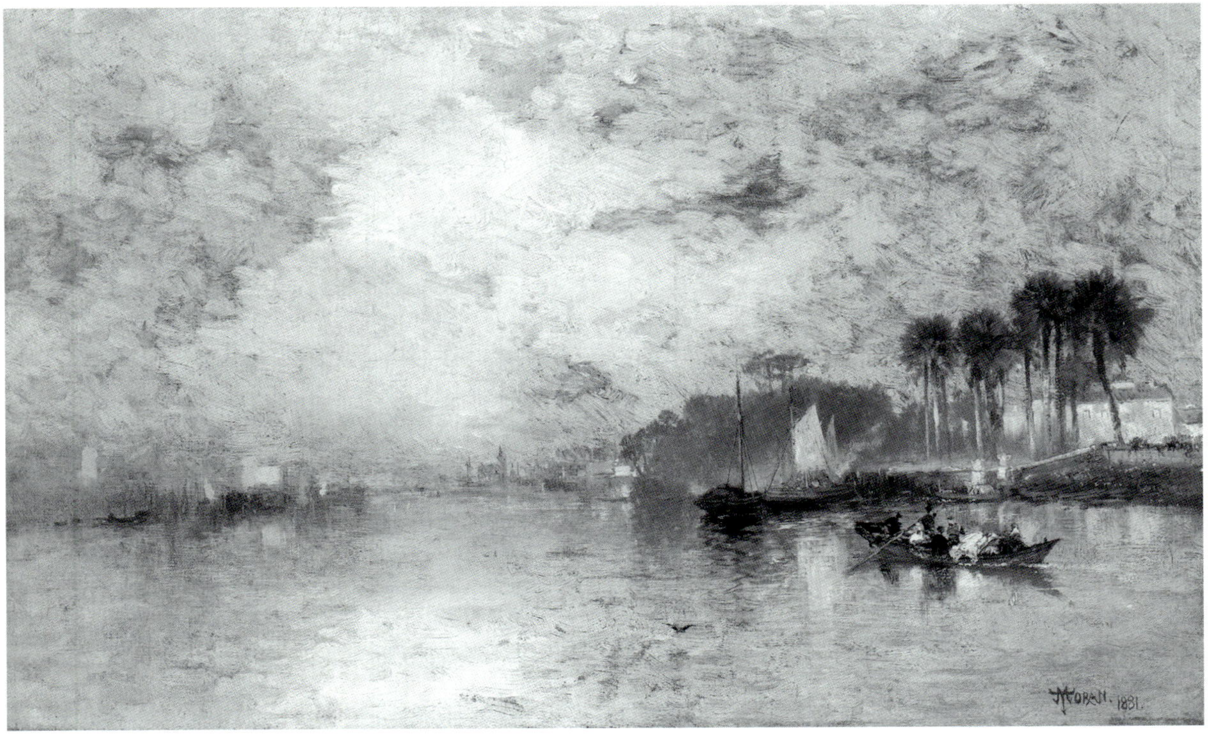

**No. 19**
Thomas Moran (1837–1926)
*On the St. John's River, Florida*, 1881
Oil on canvas, 10 x 16 in.
Private Collection

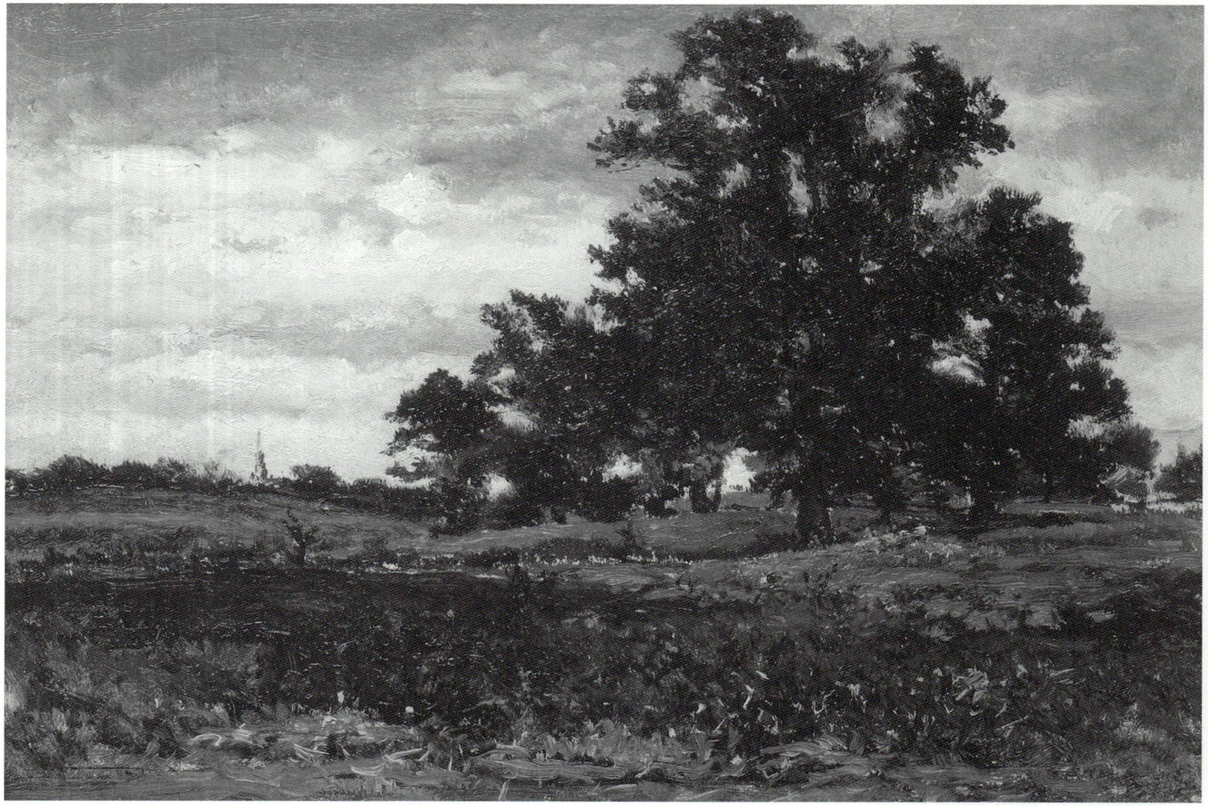

**No. 20**
George Inness (1825–1894)
*Medfield Landscape*, c. 1862
Oil on paper mounted
on board, 10.25 x 14.5 in.
Collection of Mark L. Brock

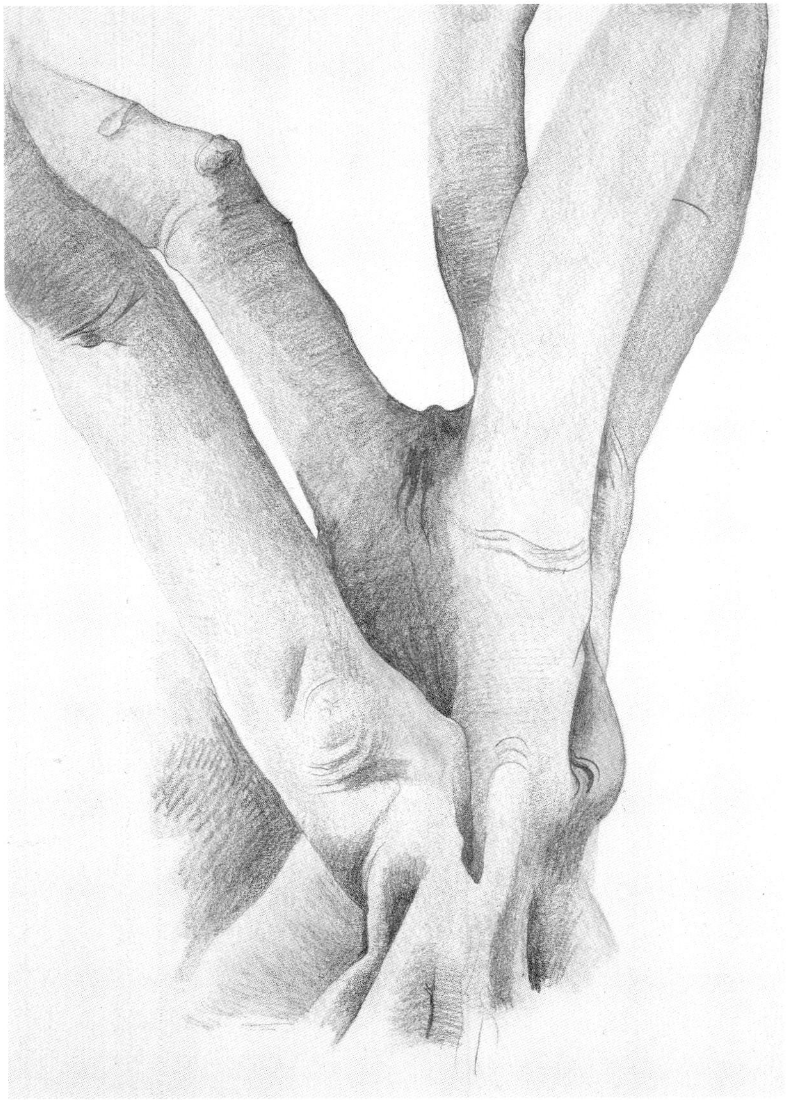

**No. 21**
Georgia O'Keeffe (1887–1986)
*Banyan Tree Trunk, Bermuda*, 1934
Pencil on paper,
21.5 x 14.75 in.
The Masterworks Foundation, Bermuda

# LIST OF WORKS IN THE EXHIBITION



Thomas Doughty (1793–1856)
*Hudson River near West Point*, c. 1835
Oil on board, 8.5 x 11.875 in.
The Montclair Art Museum, 1959.2
Gift of Mr. and Mrs. John C. Cattus

Thomas Doughty (1793–1856)
*In the Catskills*, 1836
Oil on canvas, 30.25 x 42.25 in.
Addison Gallery of American Art
Phillips Academy, Andover, Massachusetts

Jasper Cropsey (1823–1900)
*Landscape*, 1875
Oil on canvas, 14.25 x 24.25 in.
The Montclair Art Museum, 1961.3
Gift of Mr. and Mrs. Stanley Golt

John Casilear (1811–1893)
*Hudson River Scene*, c. 1850
Oil on board, 9 x 12.5 in.
Collection of Mr. and Mrs. Alec H. Petro

Hiram Torrey (1820–1900)
*Sunrise Among the Mountains*, c. 1857
Oil on canvas, 34.25 x 51.2 in.
McMullen Museum of Art, Boston College
Gift of Mr. Thomas J. Murphy, in memory of his father

Benjamin Champney (1817–1907)
*Mote Mountain from Walker's Pond*, 1878
Oil on canvas, 33 x 28 in.
Private Collection—Boston College Alum

George Loring Brown (1814– 1889)
*View of Norwalk Islands, Norwalk, Connecticut*, 1864
Oil on canvas, 21.25 x 43.25 in.
Addison Gallery of American Art
Phillips Academy, Andover, Massachusetts

Sanford Gifford (1823–1880)
*Lake Scene—Mountain Background*, 1867
Oil on canvas, 5.75 x 10.375 in.
Addison Gallery of American Art
Phillips Academy, Andover, Massachusetts
Bequest of Candace C. Stimson

Elihu Vedder (1836–1923)
*Peasant Girl Spinning*, c. 1867
Oil on canvas, 11.5 x 13.5 in.
McMullen Museum of Art, Boston College

John Enneking (1841–1916)
*Mountain Stream*, 1876
Oil on canvas, 22.25 x 14.125 in.
McMullen Museum of Art, Boston College

Martin Johnson Heade (1819–1904)
*Sailing by Moonlight*, c. 1870–1875
Oil on canvas, 14.25 x 22.25 in.
Private Collection

Martin Johnson Heade (1819–1904)
*Low Clouds over a Marsh*, c. 1895–1904
Oil on canvas, 4.75 x 8.5 in.
Private Collection

James Hart (1808–1901)
*Pasture in Early Evening*, 1880
Oil on canvas mounted on board, 18.25 x 30.25 in.
McMullen Museum of Art, Boston College

Thomas Moran (1837–1926)
*On the St. John's River, Florida*, 1881
Oil on canvas, 10 x 16 in.
Private Collection

William Sonntag (1822–1900)
*Camping by the Pond*, c. 1886
Oil on canvas, 12.125 x 20 in.
McMullen Museum of Art, Boston College

George Inness (1825–1894)
*Medfield Landscape*, c. 1862
Oil on paper mounted on board, 10.25 x 14.5 in.
Collection of Mark L. Brock

George Inness (1825–1894)
*Summer Landscape*, c. 1864
Oil on board, 8 x 16 in.
Collection of Mr. and Mrs. Alec H. Petro



George Inness (1825–1894)
*Autumn Landscape*, c. 1870
Oil on canvas, 12 x 20 in.
Private Collection—Boston College Alum

George Inness (1825–1894)
*Old Aqueduct, Campagna, Rome*, 1871
Oil on paper mounted on board, 8.75 x 13 in.
The Montclair Art Museum, 1953.38
Gift of Mrs. Eugene G. Kraetzer, Jr.

George Inness (1825–1894)
*Sunset Glow*, 1883
Oil on paper mounted on board, 16 x 24.125 in.
The Montclair Art Museum, 1946.1
Gift of Francis M. Weld

George Inness (1825–1894)
*Late Afternoon*, c. 1884
Oil on canvas, 18 x 24 in.
Collection of Mr. and Mrs. Alec H. Petro

Dwight Tryon (1849–1925)
*Twilight at Auvers*, 1878
Oil on canvas, 20.25 x 30 in.
The Montclair Art Museum, 1915.43
Gift of William T. Evans

Charles Knapp (1822–1900)
*Landscape with Water, Trees, and Mountains*
Oil on canvas, 19 x 35 in.
McMullen Museum of Art, Boston College
Gift of George Pearce Leyland
and Mary Cahill Leyland, in memory
of Kenneth Leyland

John La Farge (1835–1910)
*Landscape in Nikko*, 1887
Oil on canvas, 13.75 x 10.25 in.
The Montclair Art Museum, 1976.22
Ethel Parsons Hunter Fund

F. Childe Hassam (1859–1935)
*Morning Calm, Appledore*, 1901
Oil on canvas, 26 x 24.125 in.
Addison Gallery of American Art
Phillips Academy, Andover Massachusetts
Gift of anonymous donor

Winslow Homer (1836–1910)
*Rocky Shore, Bermuda*, 1900
Watercolor on paper, 14 x 21 in.
Museum of Fine Arts, Boston
Bequest of Grenville H. Norcross

Winslow Homer (1836–1910)
*S.S. Trinidad, Bermuda*, 1901
Watercolor on paper, 14 x 21 in.
The Masterworks Foundation, Bermuda

Winslow Homer (1836–1910)
*Inland Waters*, 1901
Watercolor on paper, 13.75 x 21 in.
The Masterworks Foundation, Bermuda

Frank Alfred Bicknell (1866–1943)
*Souvenir of Bermuda*, 1894
Watercolor on paper, 5.125 x 9.5 in.
The Masterworks Foundation, Bermuda

Evelyn Bicknell (1857–1936)
*Hamilton*, c. 1914
Watercolor on paper, 8.5 x 14.125 in.
The Masterworks Foundation, Bermuda

Ross Sterling Turner (1847–1915)
*Fairylands, Bermuda*, 1890
Watercolor and gouache on paper, 18 x 15.5 in.
The Masterworks Foundation, Bermuda

Ross Sterling Turner (1847–1915)
*Bermuda*, 1894
Watercolor and gouache on paper, 11.5 x 18 in.
The Masterworks Foundation, Bermuda

Prosper Senat (1852–1925)
*On Paget Drive*, c. 1921
Oil on canvas, 23.25 x 36.25 in.
The Masterworks Foundation, Bermuda

Prosper Senat (1852–1925)
*Pilot Boats, St. George's, Bermuda*
Oil on board, 14.5 x 9.5 in.
The Masterworks Foundation, Bermuda

Thomas Anshutz (1851–1912)
*View of Bermuda, South Shore*, 1911
Oil on canvas, 7.375 x 9.5 in.
The Masterworks Foundation, Bermuda

Charles Hawthorne (1872–1930)
*Early Morning, Bermuda*, 1928
Watercolor on paper, 13.75 x 20 in.
The Masterworks Foundation, Bermuda

E. Ambrose Webster (1869–1935)
*Cactus*, 1915
Oil on canvas, 19.5 x 23.75 in.
The Masterworks Foundation, Bermuda

E. Ambrose Webster (1869–1935)
*Blue Aloe*, 1916
Oil on canvas, 19.25 x 23.5 in.
The Masterworks Foundation, Bermuda

Houghton Cranford Smith (1887–1983)
*Bermuda Houses by Water*, 1912
Oil on canvas, 14 x 16 in.
The Masterworks Foundation, Bermuda

Houghton Cranford Smith (1887–1983)
*House with Red Amaryllis, Bermuda*, 1929
Oil on canvas, 14.75 x 20 in.
The Masterworks Foundation, Bermuda

Carl Sprinchorn
*Bermuda Beach*, 1929
Watercolor on paper, 15 x 22.25 in.
The Masterworks Foundation, Bermuda

John Lyman (1886–1960)
*St. George's, Bermuda*, c. 1920
Oil on canvas, 10.2 x 27.75 in.
The Masterworks Foundation, Bermuda

John Lyman (1886–1960)
*Bermuda Landscape*, c. 1930
Oil on canvas, 16 x 24 in.
The Masterworks Foundation, Bermuda

Jack Bush (1909–1977)
*Bermuda, Fort St. Catherine*, 1934
Watercolor and pencil on paper, 7.75 x 9.25
The Masterworks Foundation, Bermuda

Jack Bush (1909–1977)
*Old Maid's Lane*, 1934
Watercolor and pencil on paper, 8.2 x 7.25 in.
The Masterworks Foundation, Bermuda

Jack Bush (1909–1977)
*House and Figure, St. George's*, 1939
Watercolor and pencil on paper, 18.5 x 24 in.
The Masterworks Foundation, Bermuda

Albert Gleizes (1881–1953)
*Les Bermudes, La Maison du Gouverneur*, 1917
Watercolor on paper, 10.25 x 8 in.
The Masterworks Foundation, Bermuda

Albert Gleizes (1881–1953)
*Les Bermudes, La Maison du Gouverneur II*, 1917
Watercolor on paper, 10.25 x 8 in.
The Masterworks Foundation, Bermuda

Charles Demuth (1883–1935)
*Architecture: Red Roof*, 1917
Watercolor and pencil on paper, 11.75 x 17.75 in.
The Masterworks Foundation, Bermuda

Charles Demuth (1883–1935)
*Trees and Houses*, 1917
Watercolor and pencil on paper, 9.75 x 13.5 in.
The Masterworks Foundation, Bermuda

George Ault (1891–1948)
*A Street in St. George's*, 1922
Watercolor and pencil on paper, 15 x 16.75
The Masterworks Foundation, Bermuda

George Ault (1891–1948)
*Behind the Bakery Shop*, 1922
Watercolor and pencil on paper, 15.5 x 11 in.
The Masterworks Foundation, Bermuda

Niles Spencer (1893–1952)
*House, Bermuda (St. George's)*, 1929
Oil on board, 13 x 16 in.
The Masterworks Foundation, Bermuda

Georgia O'Keeffe (1887–1986)
*Banyan Tree Trunk, Bermuda*, 1934
Pencil on paper, 21.5 x 14.75 in.
The Masterworks Foundation, Bermuda

Marsden Hartley (1877–1943)
*Sunken Treasure*, 1935
Oil on board, 18 x 24 in.
The Masterworks Foundation, Bermuda